Canyon
Naturalists

INTERPRETING FOR PARK VISITORS

William J. Lewis

Designed and illustrated

by Keith L. Hoofnagle

EASTERN ACORN PRESS

Eastern National Park & Monument Association promotes and aids the historical, scientific, and educational activities of the National Park Service. As a nonprofit cooperating association authorized by Congress, it makes interpretive material available to park visitors by sale or free distribution. It also supports research, interpretation, and conservation programs of the Service. Eastern Acorn Press is the imprint of Eastern National Park & Monument Association.

Library of Congress Cataloging in Publication Data

Lewis, William J
  Interpreting for park visitors.

  Bibliography: p.
  1. National parks and reserves—Interpretive
programs—United States. 2. National parks and
reserves—Interpretive programs. I. Title.
SB482.A4L48   790'.06'8   80-13321
ISBN 0-89062-079-2

Produced by the Publishing Center for Cultural Resources.

Manufactured in the United States of America.

TABLE OF CONTENTS

Shows how to involve park visitors in interpretation by using: their knowledge and interests, questions, all the senses, and structural variety. Also shows how to develop oral messages for park visitors by giving attention to: topic choice, themes, theme development, delivery, accuracy, and safety.

Emphasis is placed on the visitor center and roving interpretation.

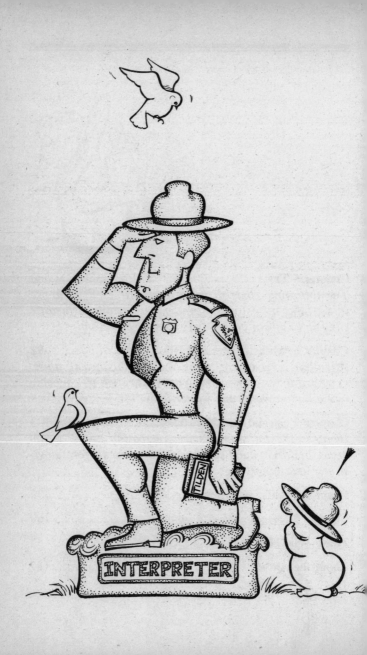

INTERPRETER

TILDEN

PART ONE
WHAT IS AN INTERPRETER?

You've received notice that you've made it, that you're going to be an interpreter for the National Park Service. Your joy is boundless! You jump up and down with happiness, connecting your ears with an expanding grin. The news is too good to keep, so you rush to share it with your nearest friend. "Guess what?! I'm going to be an interpreter for the National Park Service!" "Oh," your friend replies, "I didn't know you spoke any foreign languages." "No, not that kind of interpreter," you reply, "but the kind that answers questions for park visitors." "Visitors from other countries?" your friend insists. "No, for everyone, people of all ages, nationalities." "Why, then, are you called an interpreter?" "Because when I take people on a tour or a walk, I'll be helping them understand what they're looking at." "Oh, I see, you're really going to be a guide."

What are you really going to do as a park interpreter? This book has been put together to help you know what's expected of you and to help you be an outstanding interpreter. Here are some examples of some things you might do as an interpreter.

You're at Whiskeytown National Recreation Area in California showing visitors how to pan for gold, and you help them find a few flakes. The experience leads to a discussion of the area, its historical significance. The tedium of the life of a searcher for gold becomes apparent, and visitors walk away with new insights into certain aspects of human history.

At Glacier Bay, you board a tour boat loaded with park visitors and spend the day talking about ice, giving a geological explanation for its presence as well as describing the effects of the ice on the flora and fauna of the area. Visitors (most of whom have arrived by jet aircraft or ship) gasp at your story of John Muir's plying of these waters in a canoe and actually living in a cabin he built in this vast wilderness. You show how people, other animals, and plant life are interdependent, and how various human activities are now affecting life in Alaska.

At Independence Hall, you quickly gather a group and hurry them through the building, knowing that another tour is right behind. There's just enough time to express some ideas about the significance of the place, to show

them where Benjamin Franklin, Thomas Jefferson and others sat, and perhaps inspire the group with a feeling of excitement and appreciation for what happened there. You help your group make a connection between the past and present, to understand the relevancy of past events to the present lives of visitors.

During a walk in the desert at Organ Pipe Cactus National Monument, you reveal some interesting facts about the kangaroo rat who never drinks water, but obtains all of its moisture from the food it eats. You explain that the rat conserves water and energy during the day by living in a hole it has dug, and which it seals up with dirt. If people would provide similar insulation, you suggest, they, too, could prevent energy loss.

The importance of one's roots comes alive as you lead a tour through Lincoln's Boyhood Home. It becomes clear that the early experiences each of us has in life play a major role in our adult behavior.

At Gettysburg, you help visitors have a feeling for war, for the lives of the men who participated in this event. Perhaps you make them wonder whether this terrible war

was necessary, and whether it did more harm than good to the country as a whole.

You demonstrate the atlatl used in spear throwing as well as arrowhead making at Russell Cave in Alabama, helping park visitors realize how difficult it was for early people to survive with only these elementary means of securing food. You philosophically point out that when one is required to spend most of one's energy obtaining food, there is little time for the development of music, art, dancing, religion, and other activities which are essential to the development of a cultural heritage. With decreasing energy supplies, you ask, will our cultural heritage be diminished?

The fire flickers and fades under a blackened dome liberally punctuated by pinpoints of light. You invite the campfire audience to join you in song and in picture. The relationship between climate and plant growth unfolds as you weave slides and narration together. Climate also affects us, you point out, helping show the close relationship between people, plants and environment.

You're in a Florida school using a felt board to explain

environmental relationships to first graders. You're telling them where energy comes from, how energy flows from the sun to green plants, to the animals that eat the plants, to the animals that eat the animals. Your presentation ends with an emphasis on the idea that most kinds of energy are limited, and the kids make "SAVE ENERGY" buttons.

You're in another schoolroom preparing children for a visit to the John Muir National Historic Site. They're going to be doing some role playing there for an overnight period, and it's your task to ready them for the experience. You assign them roles as field hands, Chinese domestic workers, cooks, herbalists, merchants, etc., and show them where they can find material to read so they can be prepared for their roles.

You're in the audio-visual room sorting, cleaning, framing and cataloguing slides. You're in the library searching for answers to questions you've been asked but to which you didn't know the answers. You're hiking the trails on your days off, having fun, but also gathering information that'll make you more effective when you're

asked for information. You're sitting in an advanced seminar for some in-depth in-service training.

A brightening sky disturbs your sleep. It's time the cows were milked, the chickens fed. You put on your costume of several generations ago and shuffle off to the barn to begin your day of demonstrating what life was once like at this location. You'll be living in the past for the edification of today's National Park Service visitors.

You're at the visitor center and a young boy, barely tall enough to peer over the counter asks: "Hey, ranger, how many little baby bears does a mother bear lay every year?" Another visitor perplexes you with "Does it ever get this hot around here?" "Why is the food so lousy at the cafeteria?" another wants to know. And, there are the inevitable questions: "Where's the bathroom?" "Where can I urinate?" "Where's the head?" "Where's the john?" "Where's the 'You know what'?" Whatever the word choice, they're the most frequently asked questions in the National Park Service.

As an interpreter, you're part of a team whose function

it is to provide not only for the enjoyment, appreciation and understanding of the park area by the public, but also to protect the park from the people and the people from the park—and each other. Included on the team are a wide variety of people such as maintenance personnel, law enforcement personnel, and an administrative staff. In park areas where concessioners provide services to the public such as housing, food and transportation, there are additional team members, for the persons who pump gas, assign rooms, drive buses, sell groceries, etc., can also support the purpose of the park.

While any member of the team may have contact with park visitors, it's the *primary* function of interpretation to be the interface between the park and those who visit it. Anytime you answer a question, give a guided tour, prevent damage to a fragile resource, enlarge a visitor's appreciation of a park value, you're helping the National Park Service accomplish its mission.

All park interpretation obviously isn't done by interpreters communicating directly with park visitors. Road-

side exhibits, visitor center displays, books, pamphlets, maps, self-guiding nature trails, movies, slide programs, etc., are inanimate members of the interpretive team.

As an interpreter, you're part of a tradition which began with the establishment of national parks. Within a year after the National Park Service was organized, an educational division was formed which prepared information circulars and cooperated with various universities that were using the new parks as educational scientific laboratories.

By 1923, interpretive facilities and programs at Glacier, Grand Canyon, Mesa Verde, Mount Rainier, Rocky Mountain, Sequoia, Yellowstone, Yosemite and Zion were sufficiently advanced that an office to coordinate and direct interpretation was established in Berkeley, California. Seven years later, this office was moved to Washington, D. C., where it has since remained.

In 1932, this office published a booklet which listed some interpretive goals which now sound remarkably current.

1. Simple, understandable interpretation of the major features of each park to the public by means of field trips, lectures, exhibits, and literature.

2. Emphasis upon leading the visitor to study the real thing rather than to utilize second-hand information. Typical academic methods are avoided.

3. Utilization of highly trained personnel with field experience, able to interpret to the public the laws of the universe as exemplified in the parks, and able to develop concepts of the laws of life useful to all.

4. A research program which will furnish a continuous supply of dependable facts suitable for use in connection with the educational program.

From *Research and Education in the National Parks*
by Dr. Harold C. Bryant and
Dr. Wallace W. Atwood, Jr.,
as quoted in *Basic Interpretive Principles—*
General Principles Underlying the Interpretive
Program, Chapter 3, Section 2, Page 3.

Today, interpretation in the National Park Service is overseen, on behalf of the Director, by a Chief of Interpretation and Visitor Services in Washington, D. C., as well as by Chiefs of Interpretation and Visitor Services in Regional Offices. Further, each park area designates someone to supervise this vital function.

From this interpretive tradition came the need for instructional materials to help interpreters improve their communication with park visitors. Over the years, a variety of pamphlets were produced on the art of giving campfire talks, guided walks, historical interpretation, etc. Some of the material from those earlier training manuals has been incorporated into this one.

In the section which follows, you'll find some basic principles that apply to *all* kinds of interpretation. In the final section, specific application of these principles is discussed. It is hoped that these materials will help you become an outstanding interpreter.

PART TWO

BASIC PRINCIPLES
OF INTERPRETATION

Interpretation requires an interpreter, an audience, and something to interpret. What do we know about these elements? This section will cover those elements common to *all* interpretation, while the next section will be concerned with other elements unique to a particular type of interpretation.

Chapter 1

The Interactive Threesome —
You, the Visitor and the Park

Perception One thing we know for sure is that every one of us sees the world uniquely. Some park visitors may see waterfalls as sources of power, antlers as trophies, historic sites as impediments to commercial development, trees as lumber, etc. Not only that, none of us continues to see the world in the same way. As we grow older, have different experiences, become acquainted with people who have different values, are exposed to scientific and historical research findings, and travel more widely, our ways of looking at the world are changed.

Furthermore, the world itself is in the process of change. New wars are being fought, mountain tops are filling the valleys, heroes and heroines come and go, species become endangered, then sometimes extinguished. Some of the environment is cut down, pushed around, filled with noxious wastes. Fossil energy sources are depleted at a dizzying pace. New products flood the supermarkets where clerks pass your coded merchandise over a scanner which not only tells you how much you owe, but prints a list of what you've bought.

Park visitors and interpreters live in an environment

saturated with media—television, movies, magazines, radio, recordings, newspapers—which are generally available to all. Old values are constantly undergoing change, revision. We're not only living in a world which is frenetic, but in which the pace will accelerate as long as energy sources and materials are abundant.

In a park area we bring together a unique interpreter, a unique visitor, and a unique world all of which are in the process of change. How can meaningful interpretation occur in such a changeable context? It will probably help if certain principles are understood. Maybe the most important of these is a recognition of where each of the three elements stand at the moment of interpretive contact. If effective interpretation is to occur, the interpreter must be aware of the in-common intersections of all three elements. This means that the interpreter must know himself/herself, the park visitor(s), and the park area itself.

What About You? Why did you choose to be an interpreter? What is there about you that's unique? What can you do in your own way that no one else can do quite as well?

Several assumptions about you were made when you were hired. Among these is that you're qualified as a person who not only knows a great deal about the subjects to be interpreted, but that you have an insatiable curiosity which ensures a continual search for additional knowledge.

It's also assumed that you have a love for all life, a regard for the incredibly complex ecology that gives special vitality to your particular park area, and for any historical objects, documents, and photographs which give insight into life as it once was, and therefore is.

Perhaps the most important assumption made about you is that you have a high regard for park visitors. You're expected to care about them, respect their values, be concerned for their welfare and safety, want them to be better informed, inspired, stimulated because of who you are. If you don't care about sharing yourself, and what you know, with park visitors, you're in the wrong job.

Caring about park visitors implies that:

1. All park visitors are entitled to your help without discrimination or distinction as to race, color, creed; whether they are famous or humble, young or old, athletic or handicapped, male or female, thoughtful or thoughtless.

2. Even when you're tired and people seem demanding and exasperating, you'll be cheerful, patient, courteous.

3. You care about your appearance whether you're in uniform or costume. Neatness and cleanliness are important criteria here. It would be unfortunate if the visitor's attention is drawn more to the way you smell than to what you're talking about.

4. You realize the appropriateness of courtesy. This is especially important when handling controversial matters such as the energy crisis, treatment of slaves, the importance of John Brown. Park visitors should not be "put down" when they ask what seem to you to be stupid questions. Starting and ending an event on time is one tangible way of showing courtesy as it indicates a respect for another's time.

5. It will be important for you to be available, approachable, sharing, and patient. You'll need to reach out to people, to start the communicative process.

It is also assumed that you are gifted with imagination, resourcefulness, originality; that you'll be sincere and enthusiastic; that you have a sense of humor that will help keep things light and in perspective; that you'll search out the facts and weave them together into a meaningful whole; that you'll understand the goals of interpretation and strive to accomplish them.

You're beginning to sound like quite a person. You are! It's important for you to have self-confidence, but also to be aware of the dangers of conceit. You're expected to show leadership without being overbearing, authoritarian. Quiet, gentle, but firm leadership is generally most appropriate.

What About the Audience? Who are the people who are lucky enough to participate in your interpretive activities? They're much like ourselves in most ways. Studies show that generally they're better educated, more curious, more widely traveled, wealthier, more sophisticated than most of the population. (In urban areas this generalization may not be as applicable. A greater variety in backgrounds may be represented at these places.) While we may wish for a more complete cross-section of people for our interpretive programs, the fact is that you will generally have a select group. More and more, they come from all over the world. They're all ages, races, nationalities. In the summer months, in most places, they're more numerous and traveling as family units. In winter, particularly in urban centers, there's a great deal of interpretation given to school groups.

You'll find a great variety of occupations represented in any interpretive group, although demographic studies show that the professions are most frequently represented. For example, one study shows that school teachers make up the largest segment of those taking nature walks in Yellowstone National Park.

Why do people participate in interpretive activities? While reasons vary considerably, some would undoubtedly include the following: (1) To learn something they otherwise wouldn't. (2) To be with someone who will communicate with them—you. (3) To make the unfamiliar familiar. (4) To have an encore to a previous interpretive experience that was good. (5) To satisfy one's curiosity. (6) To experience bodily exercise while learning. (7) To learn how to learn more. (8) To meet other park visitors in a relatively intimate setting. (9) To find new insights, relationships, relevancies. (10) To relax. (11) To have an aesthetically pleasing experience. (12) To be touched, moved, inspired. (13) To experience provocation, as well as instruction. (14) To appreciate the uniqueness of the park site. (15) To find someone else to amuse the kids for awhile. (16) To have their pictures taken with the interpreter to show folks back home how they spent their vacation. (17) To be amused.

It can be seen from this listing that park visitors come to interpretive activities with definite expectations. They're already in your corner. But you also have a very high challenge, because, as you can see, their expectations are very high. It's up to you to meet their expectations, to exceed them if you can.

How do people learn? Since learning is such an important part of the interpretive process, it will be worthwhile to examine some basic assumptions which are commonly accepted about learning. These assumptions are adapted from various National Park Service publications including: *Environmental Study Area Workshops, National Park Service Training Methods Manual,* and *A Personal Training Program for Interpreters.*

1. People learn better when they're actively involved in the learning process.
2. People learn better when they're using as many senses as appropriate. It is generally recognized that people retain about
   10% of what they hear
   30% of what they read
   50% of what they see
   90% of what they do
3. Each person has unique and valid ways of processing information and experience.
4. New learning is built on a foundation of previous knowledge.
5. People prefer to learn that which is of most value to them at the present moment.
6. That which people discover for themselves generates a special and vital excitement and satisfaction.
7. Learning requires activity on the part of the learner.
8. Friendly competition stimulates learning.
9. Knowing the usefulness of the knowledge being acquired makes learning more effective.

10. People learn best from first-hand experiences.

11. People learn best when an experience is close to them in time and space.

12. An organized presentation is more memorable than an unorganized one.

13. Increasing the ways in which the same thing can be perceived helps people derive meanings.

14. Questions can be effectively used to help visitors derive meanings.

15. Giving visitors expectations at the beginning of an interpretive activity will focus attention and thus improve learning.

16. Using a variety of approaches will enhance learning.

17. The ways in which interpreters respond to people will affect their learning.

There's one more factor to be discussed. Then we can put together what we know about you, the visitor and the park area into a plan of action.

Something To Interpret The National Park Service administers nearly 300 areas. Each of them has been set aside because it has something unique about it. Some of the variety in the type of area has been indicated in the opening section. When people come to a National Park Service area, they're entitled to know what the special things about it are. People don't want to travel all the way from Florida to Mt. Rainier National Park to hear a lecture on water pollution. They've either heard it before or don't need the setting of Mt. Rainier to hear it now. What special events occurred at Fort Clatsop, at Fort Vancouver? How is the Olympic National Park different from its near neighbor the North Cascades National Park? What's special about the Lake Chelan National Recreation Area?

Not only should each park unit have a unique theme, but its subdivisions should have their separate stories. At Independence National Historical Park, for example, Carpenter Hall, the Liberty Bell, Franklin Court, the First and Second Banks of the United States, and Independence Hall all have unique differences which require unique interpretation. In Yellowstone National Park, the themes at the Yellowstone Lake, the Grand Canyon of the Yellowstone, and the geyser basins should all emphasize their differences. At the same time you're emphasizing the differences, however, you should also point out the ways in which all of the parts interrelate.

Now that we have an interpreter, an audience and something to interpret, what are we going to do? What are the goals of interpretation? How do we go about it?

[For a review of this chapter, see questions 1 through 23 in Chapter 8.]

Chapter 2

Goals of Interpretation

Much has been written about the purposes of interpretation. Here are some of the more commonly agreed upon goals as expressed by interpreters. You will see that they are quite similar to the goals of the visitors. (1) To help park visitors understand that the place they're visiting is related to the place they call home. (2) To help visitors understand the interrelationships among as many aspects of what is being observed as possible. (3) To help visitors have an inspirational, relaxing, good time. (4) To arouse curiosity and sometimes satisfy it. (5) To conserve park resources through an understanding and consequent appreciation of them. (6) To provide visitors with an escape from the pressures which assault them. (7) To show the relationship of what is being observed (experienced) to the lives of the observers. (8) To give the kind of interpretation which will encourage visitors to figure some things out for themselves. (9) To give accurate, interesting information which forms the foundation for an interpretation of data.

Goal Implementation We now have goals for interpretation from two points of view—the interpreter and the visitor—and we also know something about how visitors learn. When these elements are put together, we find certain items referred to several times. In the next section, these primary elements will be discussed.

[For a review of this chapter, see questions 24 and 25 in Chapter 8.]

Chapter 3

Primary Elements of Interpretation

INVOLVEMENT. Did you note how often the park visitor was involved in the examples of interpretation cited in the opening section? Visitors were panning for gold, making relevant connections between past and present, doing role playing, becoming part of an historic scene, using atlatls to throw spears, singing at campfire programs, making "SAVE ENERGY" buttons, asking questions.

Involving the visitor in interpretation is vital and can be accomplished in a variety of ways. Here are some suggestions:

What To Do First When you arrive at the place where the activity you're conducting is to take place, begin getting acquainted with your group. You find out who they are, why they're there, what special interests or backgrounds they may have that are relevant to that which is being interpreted. You establish a rapport that will encourage more intimate give-and-take. You let the visitors know who you are, what your special contributions can be. You establish the mood, the framework within which the interpretation will take place. In any interpre-

tive situation, what is first communicated is absolutely vital to that which follows.

Making Use of Visitors' Knowledge and Interests If, at the beginning of your activity, you find out what the interests of your group are, what kind of work they do, you can incorporate this information into your presentation. A pharmacist, for example, could probably comment on the use of plants in medicine, someone interested in history could perhaps tell how earlier peoples were more dependent on plants for medicines, an engineer could comment on the structure of an historic building. As you proceed with the activity, you could ask mothers how they think particular living conditions would have affected the way they dressed their children, cooked their meals, did their shopping. (The assumption is that the role of "mother" was more clearly defined in times past.) A barber in your group might be especially interested in the Old Man's Beard lichen; a truck driver in the logistical problems of keeping armies supplied, or transportation of goods from coast to coast in the 1800's; or a minority person might want to know the role his/her ethnic group played at an historic site.

Use of Questions Questioning can encourage involvement and is accomplished in three primary ways: (1) by asking questions, (2) by encouraging visitors to ask questions, and (3) by your manner in replying to questions which are asked. If you are going to encourage visitors to ask questions, you'll need to emphasize this in the early part of your presentation. Otherwise, you'll set a didactic pattern and the group will tend to become dependent on you for all the answers. Once this mood is set, it's almost impossible to change it.

When you encourage visitors to ask questions, you'll find out what they really want to know, and you'll get some feedback on how you're coming across. This will make every presentation different, a key factor in keeping things fresh.

When you ask questions, it's important to keep in mind that you should have given the visitors enough data so they can put it together to come up with the answers. Visitors must not be given the impression that they're back in the classroom having to answer exam questions. Any good technique of interpretation can be overdone.

If, after your group has begun to ask questions, you put down someone's question by implying it's a poor question, you'll likely shut off the questions that would otherwise have been raised. It's important to remember that there is no such thing as a dumb question. All questions asked are worth the time it takes to answer them.

Many helpful suggestions on the use of questions in interpretation are given in *A Personal Training Program For Interpreters,* pp. 27–56.

Using All the Senses Giving someone the opportunity to grind corn as former inhabitants of Mesa Verde did; to write with a quill pen; to smell and taste various plants (when doing so will not negatively deplete the resource);

to experience the foods of another era; to handle replicas of historic objects; to safely feel steam-heated ground in a geyser basin; and to smell the characteristically sweet syrupy odor which is given off by plants in newly steam-heated ground; to tactily explore the stress lines on a rock outcropping; to try fly fishing; to sketch one's surroundings; to paddle a canoe; to be temporarily locked in an isolation cell at Alcatraz; to taste watermelon snow; to run one's hands through various soils; to lie on one's back on the ground experiencing the sun as a plant does; to wade through the waters of the Everglades; to feel the spray from a waterfall or an ocean breaker; all of these things—and more—will encourage involvement.

For additional ideas on sensory awareness, see Steve Van Matre's two books: *Acclimatization: A Sensory and Conceptual Approach to Ecological Involvement* and *Acclimatizing: A Personal and Reflective Approach to a Natural Relationship.*

Variety Through Structure The way your group is structured will affect involvement. If all the interpretation is going from you to your group (didactic structure), you'll obviously have less involvement than if you use a small group structure in which you divide your large group into smaller groups of 4–6 to accomplish a task. In the small group situation, everyone has more opportunity to participate—to be involved. On an historical tour, or on a walk through a natural area, for example, you might ask each small group to imagine that they're early explorers in the area and that they're going to have to make a report to their sponsor when they return home. The task for each group would be to decide what should be in the report. This could be a major or minor part of the interpretive activity.

After taking a group on a tour of some of the prehistoric ruins of the Southwest, during which the focus was on the lifestyle of these early inhabitants, it would be involving to use small groups to work on the task of planning a tour to be given several hundred years hence through the ruins of our present civilization.

Other useful, involving structures include (1) individual task structure, (2) tutorial structure, (3) conference, (4) group meeting, (5) Socratic structure. Individuals might be given hand lenses to discover hidden patterns in nature or to find hidden clues in faded documents, or compasses could be distributed and each individual could be asked to work out an orienteering problem. If help is given in accomplishing these tasks, the structure becomes tutorial.

A conference can be used whenever you want the group to have a break, to talk or explore as a group without any agenda imposed on them. This might be at any aesthetically pleasing spot in a natural surrounding, or at an historic site where one has the choice of several things to observe at once. The interpreter doesn't interfere with the process.

If there's a problem to be solved, a group meeting might be held to examine the possible causes and cures for the problem. The interpreter leads the discussion to the extent that guidance is given in the form of information, clarification of issues, etc. The burro problem of the Southwest, the encroachment of civilization on the Everglades, the protection of endangered species, the handling of increasing numbers of visitors to national park areas are all representative of the sort of problem a group meeting might be given to discuss.

The Socratic structure is used when an interpreter wishes to clarify an issue or enhance an idea by asking questions or posing problems for a group. There is an open exchange of ideas which are probed, refocused, diagnosed. The interpreter plays a major role in leading the discussion and knows the answers s/he wants to elicit. This method is especially useful for handling controversial subjects such as slavery, treatment of the Native Americans, the environment.

For a more complete discussion of the structures, see *A Personal Training Program for Interpreters,* pp. 65–87.

ORGANIZATION Regardless of the kind of interpretation you'll be doing, you'll need to be organized. This will help prevent the meandering, purposeless, scattered presentation that can occur in interpretation. Sometimes interpreters subject their audiences to a rambling series of unrelated facts. The following procedures will help you as you assemble the parts of your presentation into a meaningful whole.

Picking a Topic The first thing to do, before making any interpretive presentation, is to pick a topic. Sometimes this will be done for you by your supervisor, but if it isn't, consider some of the things we've already talked about: yourself, the audience and the site you'll be interpreting. Topics might include things like (1) plants, (2) historical relevancy, (3) geology, (4) ecology, (5) life—then and now, (6) swimming. These topics are obviously very general. Since it's difficult to cover broad topics effectively, it's necessary to narrow the topic, to establish some focus. That's where the theme comes in.

Choosing a Theme One of the most important tools in interpretation is the theme. Used properly, it can be the key to effective organization. At the completion of any interpretive presentation, the audience should be able to tell you what was said by summarizing it in one sentence. This sentence is the theme, the central or key idea of any presentation. Development of a theme provides both organizational structure and clarity of understanding. Once the theme of a presentation has been chosen, everything else tends to fall into place. A theme should:

Be stated as a short, simple, and complete sentence.
Contain only one idea.
Reveal the overall purpose of the presentation.
Be specific.
Be interestingly and motivatingly worded when possible.

There are several advantages to using a theme. One of the most important of these is that it limits the subject being covered, and thus encourages unified, in-depth interpretation. The use of a theme can steer you away from such things as: mere ticking off of dates, giving lists of happenings, making identifications with no reference to context. By wording a theme, you narrow and refine your topic.

Here are some themes for you to consider. You'll note that they could be used in a variety of interpretive settings.

- Most living things are dependent on the sun.
- Several important events occurred at Independence Hall.
- Boating safety involves several considerations.
- Everything is becoming something else.
- The mosquito plays an important role in nature.
- Geyser function is dependent on 3 variables.
- Lincoln's life was often marred by tragedy.
- The grizzly's survival is threatened by several factors.
- The Battle of Antietam changed the focus of the war to freedom for the slaves.

- Water is both building and "destroying" Mammoth Cave. (Can a natural event be called destructive? Is destruction simply a step on the road toward construction?)

Once you've worded your theme, its development becomes the major portion of the presentation. Suppose you were to use the theme about geyser function from the previous list. Your presentation would obviously have three parts: geyser function is dependent on (1) heat, (2) water, and (3) the right kind of plumbing system. Or, suppose the theme of your presentation is the one on the Battle of Antietam. You could point out that the Battle of Antietam greatly altered the course of the Civil War because: (1) it ended Lee's first invasion of the North, (2) it postponed indefinitely England's threatened recognition of the Confederacy, and (3) it gave Lincoln the opportunity to issue the preliminary Emancipation Proclamation.

Developing the Theme It is often helpful to outline the structure of a presentation you're going to make. The overall structural pattern for a presentation usually looks like this:

I. Introduction
II. Theme
III. Theme development
IV. Conclusion

Attention will be given to introductions and conclusions later. Right now, let's take a look at theme development by using the geyser theme referred to earlier. In outline form, the theme development would begin to look like this:

I. Introduction
II. Theme: Geyser function is dependent on three variables.
III. Theme development:
    a. A geyser needs lots of heat.
    b. A geyser requires water.
    c. A geyser must have a constricted plumbing system.
IV. Conclusion

It's obvious that the initial development is derived directly from the theme itself. The three sentences (A, B, C) above are called main headings. Main headings will be most useful if they:

- Are stated as short, simple and complete sentences.
- Do not exceed three or four in number.
- When added together, equal the theme.
- Are interestingly and motivatingly worded.

Once you've established your main headings, the next step is to develop each of them. Continuing with the geyser example, your outline might now look like this:

A. A geyser needs lots of heat.
  1. The heat is volcanic in origin.
  2. The heat source is buried thousands of feet beneath the earth's crust.
B. A geyser requires water.
  1. Most of a geyser's water originally fell to earth as snow, rain, hail, etc.
  2. Some of the geyser's water comes directly from the magma which underlies a geyser basin.
  3. The route the water follows to get into a geyser's plumbing is complex.
C. A geyser must have a constricted plumbing system.
  1. Bunsen first explained geyser function when he used constricted tubing.
  2. The plumbing of a geyser follows cracks and fissures in the earth's crust.
  3. These cracks and fissures must be lined with a hard mineral precipitated out of the geyser water.

This is only the skeletal outline of a theme development. The items under the main headings are called subheadings, and are developed by the use of such devices as examples, illustrations, quotations, visuals (when appropriate), anecdotes, and stories. The use of this type of supporting material will be discussed in a later section.

If you were developing the geyser function theme, would it make any difference whether you talked about heat, water or plumbing first? Probably not. When it doesn't matter in what order you take up the main headings, the arrangement is called **topical.**

In some cases, however, the order in which the main headings are developed does make a difference. The development of some historical themes, for example, could follow a **chronological** order. Development of the Independence Hall, Lincoln and Battle of Antietam themes referred to earlier could be developed according to when they occurred in time. Geological themes often use this pattern as well. But not all historical themes need be treated chronologically. The tragedies in Lincoln's life, for example, could be developed by working from smaller to larger tragedies, using a **climactical** order. Or the tragedies could be treated topically if none of the tragedies is seen as any worse than any other.

Another way to arrange main headings is **spatially**. The Battle of Antietam could be considered spatially, for example, by pointing out army locations and strategic maneuvers. This order could also be used, for example, to show the spatial relationships of the main house to the outlying buildings at George Washington's birthplace. The habitats of plants could also be developed spatially as you explain why a plant grows one place instead of another.

Main headings may also be arranged by **process** order. Most demonstrations would be arranged in this way. The making of sorghum molasses, for example, is a process which requires certain events to take place in a definite sequence. The same holds true for topics such as crop growing, basket weaving, and pottery making.

Obviously, there are many ways for you to give order to the main headings in your presentation. You'll have to decide which is best for you in any particular situation. The important thing is to have an order that is consistent, and that enhances the material you're presenting.

The Introduction After you've planned the basic structure of your presentation, it's time to decide how you're going to begin. Introductions will vary somewhat depending on whether you're leading a tour, guiding a walk, giving a campfire talk, etc., but they all have certain characteristics in common. An effective introduction will (1) create a favorable atmosphere, (2) arouse interest in your subject, (3) clarify the purpose of your presentation.

You Can Create a Favorable Atmosphere If You:

Refer to Current Interests of the Audience There might be some item in the news which has attracted a lot of attention to which you could refer. The news is full of examples of struggles for power ranging from political power to athletic power. Reference to such an event, taking care not to show where your preferences lie, might lead into subjects dealing with political power in the past compared to now, the struggle for supremacy among animals, plants—a never-ending contest. Or the current interest of the audience might be in the mosquitoes that have been biting them all day. Reference to this interest might effectively lead into a discussion of the notion that all things are important in life, that life is a complex balance of interdependencies, that people aren't always at the top of the food chain.

Respond to the Mood of Your Audience Prior to beginning your presentation, you should become acquainted with your audience. You can then adapt to the mood of the group. If they're in a light mood, you can respond with humorous banter (hopefully). If they're in an inquisitive mood, you can respond by giving them some unusually interesting information. If they're in a hostile mood, your introduction will have to be longer than usual as you will need to have your audience in a receptive mood before proceeding.

Refer to the Special Interests of the Audience All visitors will want to know how to get the most out of their visit to your area. You can help them know what their options are by suggesting some thing they might do. If you're in a natural area and have campers in your audience, they'll want to know how safe camping is and where the best campsites are.

Honestly Compliment the Audience By their very presence, park visitors have shown a special interest in your presentation and are probably very supportive of the necessity of preserving the kind of areas which are administered by the National Park Service.

You can arouse interest in your subject by:

Asking One or More Stimulating Questions Did you know, for example, that the mosquito is an important pollinator of plants; that the male mosquito will never bite you; that the principal diet of the mosquito is plant liquids.

Using an Unusual Statement If the female mosquito can't find a source of blood from which to extract the protein it needs to make its eggs, it absorbs protein from its wings, crippling itself, but providing for the continuation of the species.

Relating a Relevant Personal Story From 1964 to 1966, bears with brightly colored ribbons in their ears were frequently seen along the west side of Yellowstone Park. The ribbons were used merely to identify the bears for a study conducted by Colorado State University in cooperation with the National Park Service. It was amazing what these colored ribbons meant to park visitors. One of the colors used was red, and many visitors concluded these were the most dangerous bears in the park. I was working at the Norris Geyser Basin that summer, and an amusing thing happened to me twice. I'm sure these people were absolutely serious, although it may be difficult to believe. Two people came up to me, on different occasions, and said, "We saw a bear down the road with a blue ribbon in its ear. What prize did it win?"

Using a Provocative Quotation Suppose your subject is water. You could begin something like this: "In *Ecclesiastes* we read, *'All the waters of the land run down to the sea yet the sea is not full, whence the waters come, thither they return again.'* Water still evaporates, falls to the earth, and runs downhill, and in this cycle from land to sea to air and back to the land, it affects the landscape, the forests, the fields of wildflowers, and the animal inhabitants of the wilderness, as well as the welfare of even those of us who live far below the mountains."

Referring to a Problem The early inhabitants of Chaco Canyon in New Mexico stripped the area so completely of trees to use in the construction of their multi-storied dwellings that the land could no longer hold back the soil when it rained. The lack of suitable soil and adequate rain combined to make the area relatively uninhabitable. Are we, today, faced with a similar problem? Could our present rate of forest utilization eventually cause us a similar problem?

Using an Illustration or Narrative As the Lewis and Clark expedition approached the area of the Missouri River that is now known as Great Falls, Montana, they were very much impressed with what they saw. Lewis wrote in his journal that Sacajawea had been dangerously ill, but that she found great relief from the mineral water of a sulphur spring which poured over a twenty-five foot precipice into the Missouri River. He also wrote:

There are vast quantities of buffaloe feeding in the plains or watering in the river, which is also strewed with the floating carcasses and limbs of these animals. They go in large herds to water about the falls, and as all the passages to the river near that place are narrow and steep, the foremost are pressed into the river by the impatience of those behind. In this way we have seen ten or a dozen disappear over the falls in a few minutes. They afford excellent food for the wolves, bears, and birds of prey; and this circumstance may account for the reluctance of the bears to yield their dominion over the neighbourhood.

Lewis, Meriwether. *The Lewis & Clark Expedition:* The 1814 edition, unabridged, vol. I. Philadelphia: J. B. Lippincott Co., 1961, p. 237.

This area, so beautifully described by Lewis, is now squatted upon by a large refinery, and the spring which restored Sacajawea to health is nowhere to be found. What is the relationship of beauty to the manufacture of needed goods? Must the relationship always be negative?

The Conclusion You can conclude your presentation in a variety of ways. You can summarize your main headings and repeat the theme. Questions can be raised as to what's next, what the future holds. With care not to over-do it, you can assume an inspirational tone and challenge the audience to be appreciative, to take action or whatever seems to be appropriate. Work to a strong, memorable final sentence and quit. Do *not* weaken the impact of your last sentence by thanking the group for coming, for their attention. This will divert attention from that last dramatic, effective moment.

See if you think that the following conclusion from a presentation about the Battle of Antietam meets the suggestions given above: "This was the war's bloodiest day. Had Robert E. Lee won a decisive victory it might have foreshadowed the final independence of the Confederacy. As it was, the battle gave President Abraham Lincoln the opportunity to issue his preliminary Emancipation Proclamation. Now the purpose of the war broadened. Not only would Lincoln fight to preserve the Union, he would end slavery as well. The bloody Battle of Antietam provided the backdrop for a great moral victory."

GIVING LIFE TO A SKELETON. You now have a skeletal outline for your presentation. It's time to put some flesh and blood on the bones. You have your choice of a wide variety of possibilities. Here, with illustrative examples, are some of the things you can do.

Choice of Supporting Material

Relate Factual Data in Support of Your Ideas Life was difficult for Lewis and Clark as they worked their way up the Missouri River. They floundered in treacherous sand and mud, struggled to push off from snags, suffered from sunstroke, mosquitoes, fierce storms, and snake bites.

Use Anecdotes and Examples Meriwether Lewis wrote in his journal that he'd rather fight two Indians than one bear. He describes one occasion when six hunters crept up on one grizzly. From a distance of only forty paces, four of the hunters fired, each scoring a hit. The bear attacked and before the foray was over, two men had been chased over a twenty-foot embankment into the river, and the other hunters completely routed. When the dead bear was examined, it had been hit eight times.

Make Comparisons and Contrasts The habitat of the water lily is quite different from that of an ocotillo which looks like a dead, thorny pole most of the year. Only when there is moisture in the desert does the ocotillo turn green and blossom.

Cite Testimony and Quotations Dr. George Marler, distinguished geyser expert, has said that the Norris Geyser Basin could be thought of as the lid of a future volcano. So, if you're camping near there, don't drive your tent pegs too deeply.

Employ Narration As Andrew Jackson's troops advanced, the Creek Indians remained very confident. After all, they were in the horseshoe bend of a river, protected on three sides by water, and by a barricade they had erected on the fourth side. Probably, the most important reason for their confidence came from the trust they had in their medicine men who had told them they would be invincible at that location. When the battle was over, their confidence had obviously not been warranted. Attacked from all four sides (some of Jackson's forces had easily crossed the river by boat) the battle soon ended with nearly 100% of the 1,000 Indians dead compared with Jackson's losses of 49 men. Are we overly confident today in a way similar to the Creek Indians? Do we believe that science will find an answer to every problem, including dwindling energy resources?

Visual Materials Slides, skulls, artifacts, maps, animal droppings, historic buildings, vistas, leaves, rocks, historic photos and paintings, etc., are all examples of the type of support material that you can use. More will be said about visual materials later in the manual.

Choice of Language.

Transitions Interpreters usually know their subjects so well they have no trouble understanding how the different parts of their messages relate to each other, but these relationships may not be clear to an audience unless transitions are effectively used. As the skeletal outline is fleshed out, it becomes essential to help the audience follow you from one idea to another.

A good transition should (1) summarize the preceding idea, (2) establish the relationship between the preceding and following ideas, and (3) preview the next idea. For example: Now that we know how water gets into a geyser, let's discover how it gets out. Or, after the battle was over, the troops settled in for a few hours of restless sleep, not knowing the events which were to occur at dawn.

Sometimes, short phrases are enough to move you and the audience from one point to another. *This suggests, in contrast to, by comparison, in the meantime, an even more interesting instance, parallel situation, at another time* are all examples of transitions that may be useful to you. They will tend to give your presentation a flow that will be easy to follow.

Understandable Words Each profession has a jargon all its own and interpreters become so used to hearing, seeing and using highly technical terms that park visitors are sometimes left in the dark. While it's better, in general, to use the layman's terms during the interpretative process, it's important not to talk down to a group. Sometimes it's helpful to use some technical language, but explain it as you use it. The term *hydrothermal* becomes a useful expression once the visitor knows it refers to hot water. *Piece, redoubt, Anasazi complex, plant succession, territoriality, fault, Sonoran life zone, saprophyte, 12-pounder,* and *scraffiti* are all useful terms, for example, if they are understood or explained to an audience. You can generally tell from the feedback you receive whether your language is at too high a technical level—or too low.

Informal Language Most of us have learned to write in a relatively formal style, but to speak informally in conversation. When the formal language of the essay, the term paper, the theme, is used in spoken form, it sounds awkward. Too often, beginning interpreters try writing out their presentations word for word which generally results in a formal style. The problem is compounded when the exact word choice becomes so important that the interpreter attempts to memorize the message. This makes the presentation even more formal and mechanical.

Use Concrete Words Overuse of abstract language will weaken the impact of your presentation. You'll be most effective if you illustrate general principles with specific, concrete language. Whenever possible use sensory appeals, images, and pictorial language. Note the language Annie Dillard uses as she describes an encounter between a frog and a giant water beetle. The beetle, having bitten the frog, has injected enzymes into it which dissolve the frog's muscles and bones and organs. Here's part of what she observed:

He was a very small frog with wide, dull eyes. And just as I looked at him, he slowly crumpled and began to sag. The spirit vanished from his eyes as if snuffed. His skin emptied and drooped; his very skull seemed to collapse and settle like a kicked tent. He was shrinking before my eyes like a deflating football. I watched the taut, glistening skin on his shoulders ruck, and rumple, and fall. Soon, part of his skin, formless as a pricked balloon, lay in floating folds like bright scum on top of the water: it was a monstrous and terrifying thing. I gaped bewildered, appalled. An oval shadow glided away. The frog skin bag started to sink.

From Annie Dillard, *Pilgrim at Tinker's Creek.*
N.Y.: Harpers Magazine Press, 1974, pp. 5-6.

DELIVERY Delivery is the physical process by which a message is transmitted. It includes such items as the way a person walks, stands, sits, gestures; the way a person uses his/her voice; visual directness; etc. It's very difficult to give advice on this subject because there are so many different ways in which messages can be delivered effectively. So much of it is an individual matter, that it's difficult to make too many generalizations. The most helpful thing you can do is to have your presentation taped (videotaped, if possible) and observe your style of delivery. Invite some of your colleagues to observe your presentation and to give you some honest feedback on how you look and sound before a group. There *are* a few general principles of delivery, however, that should be helpful to you.

Be Enthusiastic Studies show that *dynamism* is one of the most important factors involved in effective communication. This should be easy for you. You're an interpreter, after all, because you love your subject matter, you have a burning desire to share what you know with the public, and you have an audience that's very much interested in what you have to say.

Use Variety While it's a good idea for you to be vigorous, forceful and driving at times, it would be a good change to have a quieter, mellow, simple, warm, earthy type of delivery.

Feel Self-Assured After all, you're the expert. You've researched your subject thoroughly, and you've organized it into a meaningful presentation which you're eager to share.

Be Physically Direct It's especially important for you to make contact with the eyes of your audience. You can learn much from this as it's an excellent source of feedback. It also gives the audience the feeling that you're interested in them.

Use Abundant Bodily Activity Although you can err by gesturing too much, especially if it's purposeless, most people are too inhibited in this respect. Good descriptive gestures not only help people visualize what you're saying with words, but they also tend to give your body a feeling of freedom by giving it something to do. Gesturing intensifies feelings within you and will enable you to be more forceful and outgoing. Planned gestures hardly ever work effectively. It's better to let them spring from the enthusiasm you're feeling for your subject.

Be Friendly, Pleasant, Informal and Casual This style of delivery is especially appropriate for interpreters as it matches the attitude most visitors bring to National Park Service areas.

Adapt Your Pace to the Situation If you can accomplish your goal in five minutes, why drag it out to ten? On the other hand, either take the time you need to develop your theme adequately, or choose a theme that will fit the time limit available. If you're sufficiently aware of the feedback you're receiving, you can generally tell whether you're going too fast or too slowly; or maybe your pace is monotonously the same. The need for variety seems to be universal, so plan for changes in your pacing.

ACCURACY Honesty is a key factor in human interrelationships. Without it, credibility suffers. The uniform you wear, the position you hold, the organization for which you work, all give you credibility. So, you're starting off your presentation with a very high degree of acceptability. If you have carefully researched your subject, you can be sure of most of your facts. The time you've spent in the library and talking with experts will pay off in accuracy as well as interest. It's impossible for anyone to know everything, but the more you know the better. When you don't know something, it's essential

that you honestly admit it. Seeking truth, rather than self-praise, means that being wrong is helpful because you've learned something new. If the audience hears you giving inaccurate information, your credibility will suffer and your presentation will be greatly weakened.

SAFETY Visitors have come to your area from familiar surroundings where they should know how to behave safely. Now, they are in an unfamiliar environment, and may not know the hazards that are peculiar to your area. Safety is an integral part of interpretation. You're especially responsible for the safety of any group while you're interpreting for them. More than that, you should always be conscious of the need for visitor safety. The *prevention* of injury or the loss of life, is better than any cure that has been devised. Visitors should be warned of dangers, and then they should be watched to make sure they follow the advice you give.

[For a review of this chapter, see questions 26 through 45 in Chapter 8.]

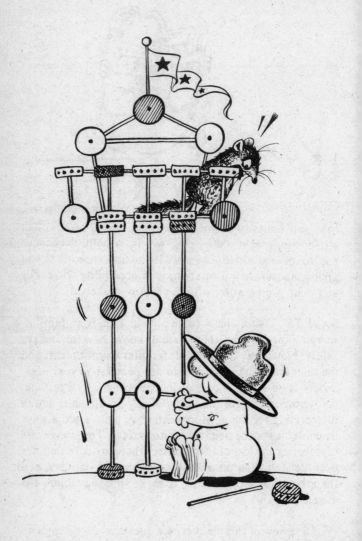

PART THREE

SPECIFIC APPLICATION OF PRIMARY ELEMENTS OF INTERPRETATION

Chapter 4

Giving Information and Orientation

GENERAL While most of the principles discussed in the preceding section apply to information giving and orienting the park visitors, emphasis and amplification will be given here to those principles which are especially applicable to particular situations.

No matter what your duty is as an interpreter, you'll be dispensing information. If you're working at a visitor center, or assigned roving interpretation, you'll be more of an information giver than an interpreter. If a visitor has an urgent need for a restroom, an explanation of what happens to the effluent is probably not particularly pertinent. In some cases, facts suffice. Other times, visitors will want to know why things are the way they are. If time allows, the visitor should be given as amplified an answer as is wanted. The key is to be sensitive enough to the visitor's needs to give the right amount. When the feedback you're getting isn't clear, ask visitors if they want to know more.

Visitors who come to park areas are faced with adjusting to unfamiliar surroundings. Adaptation to a new environment can be very threatening. Change is often the

most terrifying of all the circumstances that befall human beings. Studies show that the death of a spouse, a divorce, a serious illness, a change of job, are among the most disturbing situations that confront us. Common to them all is *change*. As park visitors are usually in unfamiliar territory, there is a threat to their usual ways of doing things. That's probably why so many of them bring so much of their environment with them in their trailers, Winnebagos, station wagons and suitcases—to ease their adjustment to the unfamiliar.

You're part of the adjustment process. Visitors who are used to having creature comforts at home are going to want to know where they can eat, drink, get gas, find ice, souvenirs, post cards, restrooms, showers, firewood, lodging, etc., etc. They'll also want to know what entertainment is available, what activities they can participate in. All of these questions are reasonable. As a matter of fact, from your point of view, there should be no such thing as an unreasonable question.

You'll be in uniform or costume which identifies you as a person who knows the answers. So, you'd better know them. You won't be able to know everything at first—no one does, but when you don't know the answer, find it, so you'll know next time. When you don't know the answer, admit it. **No** information is better than **inaccurate** information. Establish the goal of learning several new facts each day. Keep a written record of facts so you'll have a reference source.

Whereas the uniform will be looked upon favorably by most visitors as a symbol of a long tradition of service to park visitors, there will be some who will be put off by the military nature of the uniform, by the symbol of authority represented by your badge. In either event, you should do the reaching out to the park visitor. Be the first to give a greeting. Show interest in the visitor. If the shoe were on the other foot, you'd appreciate a friendly greeting at an unfamiliar place. You'd like to feel that you were welcome.

Whether you're at a visitor center or doing roving interpretation you should be approachable. This means that you must be aware of the presence of others, and be willing to include them in whatever you're doing. If you're standing with your back to a group, reading a book, engrossed in a seductive encounter, smoking a cigarette, gazing vacantly into the distance, you're not very approachable. You'll be more approachable if you can be empathetic to the visitor's situation. Perhaps there's been a family fight, or the food at the coffee shop not only tasted awful and was expensive, but the service was poor. Moreover, the clutch on the car may be starting to slip, and the tread seems to be melting off the tires. If you're approachable, and you make things better for the visitor, it's something you can feel good about.

VISITOR CENTERS Just as you need to be personally

well groomed, so does your station at the visitor center need to have that "cared for" look. Cleanliness and orderliness of your surroundings will probably make you more approachable. Before you say a word, your appearance and surroundings have already spoken for you.

Greet people as they approach you. The temptation is to suggest that you smile, but that's an outward manifestation of an inner feeling, and there's nothing phonier than pretended friendliness. If you're genuinely friendly, an appropriate response will come. Pleasant words reflecting interest in visitors can brighten your day as well as theirs. It's only common courtesy, if you're seated, to stand when a visitor comes up to you.

Many of the people who approach the information desk in visitor centers want the same information. If there's a large group of people waiting for service, speak a bit louder than you normally would to one person so all can hear. In this way you service several at the same time, as long as you take care to give full attention to the person who asked in the first place.

Some people ask questions in visitor centers just

because they're lonely. Most of us feel better about ourselves if someone has shown some interest in us, so you can provide a valuable service. But what do you do with the person whose needs are so great they won't let you move to the next person? It's essential that you manage your service so as to give a fair share of attention to everyone. You may need to tell the visitor (pleasantly and without offense) that others must also be served and suggest that s/he wait until you can spend more time with him/her.

It's easy to make fun of some of the questions asked by visitors, to derisively laugh at, what seems to us, bizarre or gauche behavior, but it's best to let this form of entertainment take place out of sight and sound of park visitors—if it must occur at all. Visitors, hearing other visitors made fun of, will surely be discouraged from asking their own questions.

The visitor center is the place where most visitors bring their complaints. Handling them effectively will be one of your biggest challenges. When you're presented with a complaint, *listen to understand*. Too often, we listen only to justify the situation which has irritated the complainant. When this happens, an argument usually follows, and this doesn't do anyone any good. An empathetic listener can do more to assuage a complaint than anything else. Most complainants just want to know that their complaint is justified and that something will be done about it. When you can rectify a situation which has caused a complaint, do it as soon as possible. If there's nothing you can do personally, the complaint should be given to someone who can deal with it appropriately. Complaints which can't be handled on the spot should be obtained in writing. Visitors should be thanked for bringing problems to your attention.

Each area of the National Park Service has its own standard procedure for referring certain types of complaints or detailed questions on policy to permanent staffers. Know your park's procedures for these situations. Be sure that the visitor knows his/her complaint will be heard by someone who will do something about it.

The flag should be raised and all arrangements necessary for the day's activities should be accomplished prior to opening time. It's essential to open on time. Time is scarce for most visitors, and they're entitled to make the best of it.

When orienting visitors, it's important for them to know where they are, which way north is. Draw sketches when you give directions, especially if the instructions are the least bit complicated. Remember that what's perfectly clear to you is often confusing for another. Answer questions as if this is the first time you've been asked even if it's the 9,999th time. After all, it's probably the first time the visitor has asked it. Listen to **all** of a question before you start to answer it even if you're sure what the question is going to be. It's only common courtesy. Learn to read maps upside-down so the visitor can look at his/her map in the "normal" way. Avoid giving too much detail when you tell someone how to get somewhere, and avoid saying "You can't miss it." No one can give directions that'll be helpful all of the time. Meanings for words are in people's minds, not in the words themselves, and since our meanings vary, our individual interpretations will differ. If in doubt as to whether someone has understood your orientation explanation, ask for a paraphrase of what you've said. You might be surprised to know what the visitor has heard.

Avoid giving facts, and facts only, when they need interpretation. Suppose someone wants to know how far it is to Johnson's Corners, and your answer is "fifty miles." The visitor may figure she can be there in about an hour unless you point out that five of those miles are straight up, that it'll be dark before she gets halfway there, and a cold front is blowing in. Or, suppose some young people ask about the summit trail. "Ten miles," you say, and as they dash for the trail, you realize that not one of them is equipped for those rugged grades. So you'd better call them back and let them know what equipment they'll need for such an enterprise.

Every park area has its own safety hazards, or special regulations that have to be followed. You can make things a lot better for the visitor, and for the park, if you take time to explain these matters in a courteous way.

ROVING INTERPRETATIONS This type of assignment ideally combines the opportunity for giving information *and/or* interpretation. Suppose you've been assigned to rove among the crowds awaiting an eruption of Old Faithful geyser. The odds are you'll be asked about the weather; for the location of the gas station, the post office, the nearest restroom; why the geyser isn't as faithful and as big as it used to be (actually, its size and faithfulness haven't changed since Yellowstone became a park); how many gallons (litres) of water are extruded each eruption; how hot the water is, etc. Some of these questions require only factual orientation, while others *could* lead to informal, spontaneous brief orientation. It's important to be able to recognize the difference and to know when to explore an idea more fully.

The same thing applies if you're roving in an historical area. Some visitors will want to know how old things are, how big this or that is, why there are so many chimneys in a single building. Others will want to know where the nearest hot dog stand is. In any case, all of these questions could be answered either factually or with interpretation. You could, for example, use the hot dog stand question as an excuse to discuss similarities and differences between past and present eating habits. You will need to develop a sensitivity to what a visitor really wants to know. Of course, sometimes the visitor doesn't know what s/he wants until a choice is presented. In any event, roving interpreters have an ideal situation in which they can either dispense information effectively, or interpret the situation in an exciting way.

[For a review of this chapter, see questions 46 through 60 in Chapter 8.]

Chapter 5

Talks

GENERAL Part Two covered the essential principles for making presentations in general. Talks have some special considerations which will be discussed here.

Before the Talk There are several things you can do prior to any talk which will make it more effective. Arrive at the talk site in plenty of time to check out all of the equipment which you'll be using to support your presentation. This includes such things as audio-visual equipment, seating arrangements, lights, and ventilation. Once you're sure everything is in a state of readiness, you can proceed to mix with the arriving audience. The informality of the speaker conversing with the audience prior to the presentation has several advantages: (1) it establishes a friendly, informal atmosphere, (2) it helps weld the audience into a responsive whole, (3) it gives you an opportunity to assess the mood of the audience, (4) it provides you with information you can use in the introduction of your presentation, (5) it helps you visualize the audience as a collection of individuals rather than as an amorphous mass, and (6) it makes it easier for you to manage the nervous tension that is present at the beginning of any talk because you move from talking with small groups to a larger group—an easier transition.

After the Talk When the talk is over, you'll want to make yourself available for further questions and discussion. This will be a time when you can get some genuine feedback on your talk, a time when you can give further service to people who are especially motivated. The announcement that you'll be around after the talk should come at the beginning of your presentation rather than at the end where it would detract from the impact of your conclusion.

The Use of Slides in Talks Slides can be excellent supporting material for the talk you've prepared. It's important, however, to realize that they only *support* the theme you've chosen to develop. If the equipment fails, for one reason or another, you can still have a meaningful presentation if you're not totally dependent on slides. Since slides are supplementary rather than primary, direct reference to them is not usually necessary. There are exceptions, however. You may want to point to something, for example, that would otherwise be missed such as the red spot on the roadrunner bird through which it absorbs heat during the daytime to sustain it at night. Or, there may be a special technique used by an historical artist that the audience would miss unless you call special attention to it. Generally, though, the slides flow smoothly along to punctuate, underline, emphasize what you're saying. The use of two projectors with a lap dissolve heightens smoothness and continuity.

Selection of slides is of paramount importance, of course. Here's where individual preference and taste come into play. While there's usually no argument that a slide should be clearly focused, or that it shouldn't be either under or over exposed, or that it should be clean and right-side-up, there's room for difference of opinion after that. You'll have to choose slides that seem most appropriate to you and then seek advice from your colleagues, supervisors and park visitors. You can generally tell from an audience's reaction how they feel about your slide choice. The main thing is to select slides that support your theme. Showing slides just because you think the photography is great is unsatisfactory.

How many slides should you show in a 30-minute talk? That depends on the subject, how many slides are available, what kind of rhythm you want to develop, etc., but as a rule-of-thumb you should have at least five slides per minute which would require 150 slides in a 30-minute talk. It should be emphasized that there may be considerable variation from this "average." It will be important for you to vary the rate of presenting these slides. Some slides can go by very quickly as they represent a cluster of support for an idea, while others will need to be on the screen longer as you begin to develop an idea. Increasing the tempo of showing slides will be especially appropriate as you approach the climax of an idea or when you summarize.

There are times when slides, accompanied by appropriate music, can tell the story better visually than you can with words and slides. For example, suppose you've been developing the notion that the National Park Idea has given us a great heritage to enjoy. Perhaps a sequence of slides showing the great variety of places administered by the National Park Service would be the best way to make the point. Or, suppose you're trying to support the notion that parks really are for the benefit and enjoyment of the people. Maybe a series of slides showing public involvement (both positive and negative) in parks would tell the story more effectively than you could with words. Consider supplementing your slides with sound effects such as bird calls, elk bugling, horses whinnying, wind howling, congested traffic, or a dramatized narration or conversation. Motion pictures also mix well with slides.

Slides should not be used for cues. Too many interpreters wait for the slide to come on the screen to remind them of what they're supposed to say next. In professional slide programs, the verbal message usually slightly precedes (1–3 seconds) the slide which then comes along and supports what has been said.

No matter what kind of talk you'll be giving you'll want to speak to the group from a place where you can be easily seen and heard. Even with the lights out during a slide presentation, it's important that you be visible. Otherwise, the whole thing might as well be recorded in advance and played automatically. If you can be heard without a public address system, avoid using it. The more natural the presentation the more effective it will be.

THE CAMPFIRE PROGRAM

Campfires stir memories of primitive use of fire for warmth, cooking, security. They bring to mind visions of families, through many periods of time, seated around their hearths in the evening telling stories, singing songs, discussing important issues. As explorers and pioneers penetrated the American wilderness, the glowing coals of their campfires comforted them. So it was quite natural, when people began coming to the newly established national parks, that campers would gather around their neighbors' fires as night fell to tell stories, sing, and enjoy good fellowship.

When nature guides arrived in the parks in the early 1920's, this impromptu custom grew into planned campfire assemblies. The tradition continues today allowing people to gather to enjoy each other's company while providing a medium for learning more about the park. The atmosphere of natural beauty, a relaxed mood, and meditation at the day's end make the campfire an ideal situation for the development of broad themes such as the philosophy of parks and their intangible values.

THE CAMPFIRE SETTING Campfire programs may be given in places ranging from the most sophisticated amphitheatre with rear screen projection to the campfire circle at the edge of a campground that is not much different from those of 100 years ago.

The Campfire Circle The campfire continues to be the focal point of this setting. Logs are usually arranged in a semi-circle to accommodate the seating of 100 people or less. With minimal artificial intrusion, this informal setting encourages a lively give-and-take exchange of ideas between the interpreter and audience. The interpreter's goal should be to maintain a spirit of informality and spontaneity without giving the impression of disorganization. You can accomplish this by making a brief presentation (about 10 minutes or so) on some aspect of the park, preferably related to the environment around the

campfire. After the presentation, questions and answers should be encouraged, as well as the sharing of experiences. A definite time limit should be set in advance as to when the program will be over. Audiences in parks tend to be very polite and will stay even after they want to go because they don't want to offend you. If you have a definite close to your program, you can invite those who want more to stay and visit with you, but the others will feel free to go.

Larger Amphitheatres In this setting, the fire is no longer utilitarian in value, but becomes a symbol of the natural scene. The fire should be kept small to emphasize the need to conserve energy. Some interpreters have lighted a candle in the firepit to indicate the need to conserve.

BEFORE THE CAMPFIRE PROGRAM BEGINS

Recorded Music Musical preludes are often played in the larger amphitheatres prior to the beginning of campfire programs. This practice lets people know that you're going to be giving a program, and, if properly chosen, can help set the mood or atmosphere you want to establish. Silence would be better than music that has nothing to do with your program, but was chosen only because it was popular. It should be played at low volume so as not to interfere with conversations among early arrivals. Nor should it be audible much beyond the perimeter of the amphitheatre. People are entitled to quietness in natural settings.

Community Singing Here's a good way to establish informality and good fellowship. If you're going to be a song leader, you'll need ample amounts of enthusiasm and self-confidence. A fair singing voice is helpful, but not essential. Primarily, you set a proper pitch, establish a suitable rhythm, and enjoy yourself. Experience is important, so try it out on your friends before making your conducting debut on stage.

You don't have to sing the entire song, but you have to start it in order to set the key and encourage audience participation. From time to time, join in to start a less familiar verse, or to whip up the tempo. Avoid drowning out the audience by the power of your sound system.

Choose familiar tunes, old standards. The campfire is no place to be teaching new songs. And, don't keep going forever. Some people will be enthusiastic about the singing, but others will be glad when it's over. Group singing should usually not exceed 5 to 10 minutes.

The Fire It's generally better to have the campfire going well in advance of program time. The sight of the fire and people gathering will attract campers or passersby who were unaware of the program. If you're going to be using slides, you'll want the fire to be embers by the time you show them so the blaze and/or smoke won't cast distracting images on the screen.

The Interview An interview can be effectively used in the pretalk portion of a campfire presentation. An "old timer," such as a settler or pioneer resident of the region or a person who visited the park at some early stage of its existence, who has a talent for telling a story, may be willing to contribute.

A noted historian, geologist, entomologist, or public figure may have some interesting things to say in a conversation with you. Local park officials also have the potential for saying some meaningful things. The superintendent may converse with you about park policy, or one of the rangers may describe rescuing people, or a member of the maintenance staff may talk with you about the energy it takes to dispose of human wastes in national parks.

Outline the interview in advance so you'll be organized. Don't spoil spontaneity by rehearsing it. Let your questions evolve from what the interviewee is saying rather than trying to follow a set list of questions.

Questions and Answers Effective question-and-answer sessions require skill on your part. You should know what kind of things visitors ask about most often and be able, by some comment or provocative statement, to invite questions from your audience. If questions are slow in coming, as they often are at first, you can usually provoke questions by saying something like "I thought surely someone would want to know what the mosquito does with the blood it extracts from you," or "I thought someone would want to know what the weather will be like tomorrow." If, after making statements like these, you'll be patient, someone in the audience will usually say, "Well, what does the mosquito do with the blood?" or "What is the forecast for tomorrow?" Once the questioning begins, there's usually no problem continuing it.

You should repeat questions for everyone's benefit if they can't be easily heard. Although answers should be kept short, you can use questions as cues to discuss principles. For example, someone may want to know whether you can gather firewood to burn. You could use this question to open the subject of keeping things natural in a national park. The weather forecast could be an opening for a discussion of the relationship of terrain and weather and why it's especially dry (wet) where you are.

If you invite questions from an audience, you must be prepared to handle some difficult, controversial issues. A solid understanding of local park and servicewide policies is required for an adequate answer. For this reason, question-and-answer sessions are not usually recommended for first-year seasonal employees.

Announcements You can be very helpful to the park visitor if you make only a few announcements. If you're suggesting activities, stick to those that are available the next day and offer to give details about them after the program. An audience simply can't remember a lot of details. Slides showing some of your recommended activities will enhance the possibility of participation.

THE TALK ITSELF Nearly everything you need to know to give the talk itself has already been covered in Part II. Be sure to review the suggestions given there thoroughly, especially Chapter Three.

A skillful speaker will make such a smooth transition from the pretalk period to the talk itself that the audience is hardly aware that a change has taken place. Somewhere along the way, you should introduce yourself. Say a few things about yourself, but avoid referring to yourself as "only a seasonal." Welcome the people to your park area and away you go.

How long should you go? Somewhere between 25–35 minutes is about right for a campfire program. With daylight savings time, it stays light so late in the summer that it's bedtime for most campers by the time you start. It's always better to leave audiences wanting a little more than to overfeed them.

AFTER THE PROGRAM A small circle of visitors will often gather about you after the program. They'll want to thank you, correct you, share experiences, ask questions. Almost inevitably someone will want to know how to get a job like yours. If the group is fairly large, you'll want to avoid the trap of spending too much time with one person. As you dispose of one question, quickly focus attention on the next inquirer, and include the group in your reply. There may be some hangers-on who will stay until the bitter end. You'll have to excuse yourself courteously so you can get on to other duty, even if that duty is some needed rest.

HISTORIC SITES

Historic sites probably require more interpretation than
natural areas. The beauty of a rain forest, a glacier-laden
mountain range, a mountainside warmed by sunflowers,
buffalo peacefully grazing, provide a kind of aesthetic
self-interpretation that's less likely to happen at an historic site.

The monument-cluttered battlefield at Vicksburg, at
first glance, gives no indication of its true significance.
Nor do most battlefields and military posts. New Mexico's Fort Union, with its Stonehenge-like remains, is
attention-getting in a bizarre and misleading way. Without interpretation, understanding and appreciation are
virtually impossible. John Muir's home at Martinez, California, is just another large old house with minimal arch-
itectural interest. It isn't until the visitor is able to visualize the Muir family living there, that the building takes
on its true significance.

As an interpreter at an historic site, you'll be giving a
wide variety of talks. In each instance it's essential that
you be *accurate, interesting*, and *relevant*.

Accuracy implies unending research into your subject
area. It means reading diaries, journals, letters; talking
with descendants of earlier people; perusing newspapers
and other publications of the period; attending historical
seminars; having rap sessions with your colleagues; reading books and scholarly journals; etc. It means you must
be able to evaluate varying reports of the same event.
Since all historical accounts are filtered through the per-
ceptions of an individual, there is some distortion in every
report of any event. As more and more historical information is uncovered, the interpretation of an event is altered.
Therefore, you must not be dogmatically certain of any
interpretation of any event. Qualifiers such as: "Based on

what we know right now . . . ." or "According to . . . ." or "It appears that . . . ." will save embarrassment when new information proves the old interpretation to be inadequate.

We're prone to look at times gone by as the "good old days," as a time when life was simpler, happier, free from the sound and air pollution of modern civilization. This nostalgic view of the past often results in a cleaned-up, selective view of history. If you're going to interpret the past accurately, you'll need to work hard to get beyond the temptation for nostalgia. A couple of good books for you to take a look at which serve as antidotes to the artificiality too common at historic sites are: *The Good Old Days—They Were Terrible* by Otto L. Bettmann (N.Y.: Random House, 1974) and *Old Jules* by Marie Sandoz (Lincoln: University of Nebraska Press, 1962).

When something you're interpreting is authentically dirty or disorderly, it's best to leave it that way, unless safety considerations preclude it. One of the most charming things about John Muir's study at his historic home is its cluttered disorderliness. Balls of crumpled waste paper lie scattered about the floor giving the impression that Muir has just squashed the paper in anger because an idea didn't express itself adequately. It looks as if he might have just walked out of the room.

How do you make things *interesting* at an historic site? One thing you do is avoid an approach which is the presentation of mere facts and dates without relevance to the people of historical time. Visually, an historic site is only architecture and landscape. It's up to you to people it, to make it come alive by helping the visitor visualize what once happened there. The scene must be recreated in some way. This can be done with living history, or with word pictures. Independence Hall, for example, can be peopled if visitors are told who sat where. A description of Benjamin Franklin being carried in and out because of his gout, or a reference to the heat that was so stifling in the chamber because of the summer season, and because secrecy demanded closed doors and windows, adds to an effective visualization of the scene. The use of letters, diaries, poetry, music of the period, will all add interest. The important thing is to humanize history. History doesn't occur in a vacuum, it happens in a context to people.

In addition to peopling the site, you'll also have to help visitors imagine what the place once looked like. The nicely mowed grass now covering what once was something else, the macadam roads where none previously existed, the encroachment of new buildings, the selective removal of old buildings, will challenge you to recreate the original scene. Hopewell Village, for example, comes across as a prettied-up nostalgic scene without the dirt and noise and "hard life" that earlier characterized it. Saugus Iron Works has none of the houses of the people who once worked there, and one of the original slave quarters at Appomattox Court House is used as a comfort station. All of these factors, and more, challenge your ability to help visitors visualize the site as it once was.

It's not enough to be accurate and interesting. The material you present must also be *relevant*. Why was the site set aside? What is the most significant thing about it? Is there a danger that too much emphasis could be put on relatively insignificant things? Is it possible, for example, to emphasize farming at Booker T. Washington Birthplace at the expense of telling the story of what it was like to be a slave there? What is the relevance of any date? What else was happening at the same time? All historical events happen within a context. None is an isolated unit. The past has a unity and needs to be considered as a whole.

What is the relevance of weapon demonstrations, for example? Is it just fun and dramatic to see the process, or could it be indicative, compared with the present, of how much less personal weapon firing has become? And, one might question the relevancey of impersonal warfare compared with that which is more personal, or the relevancy of violence in a world where it's possible for all of its parts to be in almost instantaneous communication with the other parts. A word of caution here. You must avoid advocacy. It's enough for you to make relevancies available, and let visitors decide which are more meaningful to them.

DEMONSTRATIONS

Perhaps you've been assigned to show the process by which sorghum molasses is made, or you've decided to show how bread was baked during George Washington's childhood. In either of these cases, you'll be giving a demonstration in order to help people understand and appreciate how something may be accomplished.

While not all demonstrations are given at fixed sites, most of them are. The later discussion of guided walks and tours, beginning on page 92, can also be applied to what is said here about demonstrations.

There are several things you should keep in mind when giving demonstrations.

1. Make sure that what you're showing is visible. Standing or sitting on a slightly elevated place will be helpful.

2. If you're showing objects, hold them in front of you (rather than off to the side) as you talk about them. In this way you can look into the eyes of the audience and

gauge whether they're understanding your message.

3. Gather the audience about you as closely as possible for better visibility and audibility. This will also give you the advantage of intimacy.

4. Go through the process in a clearly organized manner.

5. Sprinkle the demonstration with light-touch humor as often as it's appropriate. Avoid the corny humor that's often used just because it's felt that humor must be used.

6. Involve the audience in the process as much as possible. When feasible, let them try the process, let them touch, smell and taste (when not prohibited by the U.S. Public Health Service).

Crafts and Skills Demonstrations What's the difference between a craft and a skill? Although somewhat arbitrary, a craft may be defined as an activity which has been learned through apprenticeship and which will be used commercially. A skill is a simpler activity learned at home, or in some other setting.

Unless you're already trained as a craftsperson, you probably won't be asked to demonstrate things like milling, weaving, blacksmithing or glass blowing. But you may be asked to learn some of the simpler skills and to make soap, bake bread, sew clothes, etc.

Regardless of whether you demonstrate a craft or a skill, remember that you should be sure that what you're doing is accurate, interesting and relevant.

Living History Role playing is an important tool of interpretation and can be effectively used by interpreters and visitors alike. As a matter of fact, when role playing is used, everyone involved takes a part. If you're playing the role of a slave on a tobacco plantation of 150 years ago, and visitors interact with you, they can't very well be their normal selves. They have to imagine it's possible to talk with someone of another period and behave accordingly. And that's all right as you really want the visitor to see your world as you're seeing it. That's what living history is all about. It's a way of getting the attention of visitors, illustrating for them *part* of the park story authentically and accurately, and leading them to look further into other interpretive areas. If you're a living history interpreter, you can't be expected to show the relevancy of the past to the present, because your role doesn't allow you the present. Someone or something else will have to develop that relevancy. You can, however, arouse interest in you as a person living in the past, and give insight into what life was once like where you are.

Good living history needs to be valid, accurate and indepth. If cotton wasn't grown at your site, or if a certain type of cooking wasn't done there, it'd obviously be foolish to portray them.

To achieve accuracy, you'll want to do things like avoiding wearing your plastic-framed eyeglasses or wristwatch with your 18th century costume, smoking 20th century cigarettes, wearing inappropriate makeup, having short hair when longer hair would be more accurate, wearing modern underclothing under a period exterior.

It will not be enough to know only about the skill or craft you're demonstrating. You'll need to know how it fit into the world of that day, as well as be conversant with the social, technical, and ecclesiastical history of the period. You'll have to know how sewage was disposed of; what newspapers, novels, poetry, and other literature people were reading; who the president and other major office holders were. It's a game, you see, and the role played by visitors allows them the privilege of trying to trip you up. Maybe your in-depth knowledge will allow you the classic kind of comeback once used by an interpreter costumed as a Civil War Union soldier. When asked "Was Grant drunk here, too?" the interpreter answered, in all seriousness and without thinking, "I don't know, sir. I'm just a corporal and he doesn't invite me to his parties."

As you can see, living history is a lot of work, but it's an effort many visitors appreciate because it brings home to them the idea that history is made by little people as well as the great. History is no longer a recitation of mere facts and dates, but a matter of men, women, and children living their lives against a backdrop of their own era, locality, and economic and social conditions. It gives the visitor a person (you) with whom they can talk, and from whom they can learn about day-to-day life of that past era. After you've whetted their appetites, they can go on to learn more from exhibits, audiovisual programs, and publications.

Is it possible for all interpreters to be effective living history demonstrators? Probably not. If you're to become

a successful demonstrator, you'll find it easier if you have certain qualifications. A never-ending curiosity about the area with which you're dealing is one. Energy and scholarship also come into play; energy to keep you constantly following the bent of your curiosity, and scholarship to prevent you from giving visitors a twisted picture of the period.

A certain amount of "ham" is essential. You should be something of an extrovert and experience as an actor helps. But discipline is needed to prevent you from becoming *the show*. Visitors are not there to see you, but to have something interpreted. You are simply the vehicle to interpret that something.

You probably won't have too much to say about your costume. Usually, it'll be provided by your supervisor who hopefully will have made every attempt to provide you with a costume that is not only authentic, but fits. But through your research, ingenuity and enthusiasm, you may come up with some authentic accessories. If you're playing the role of a trapper, you may discover a variety of traps, as well as various decorations for the

basic costume. A beaver killed by a visitor's car may give you the opportunity of discovering what it's like to skin out and prepare a pelt. The accessories must be as authentic as the basic costume, of course.

One final thought about costumes: when you're in costume, you are a demonstration, and must always be available for conversation with visitors.

If you do living history, you'll be a period actor only for the period of your assigned duty, and then it's back to indoor plumbing, television, air conditioning, wash-n-wears and the other conveniences of this century. If you lived entirely in the past, you'd be thought to be a little strange. It's important to remember that, as an interpreter, you're re-creating the past, not creating it.

You'll sometimes be part of a larger scene at places where living history encompasses the whole site. The entire area will be populated with interpreters playing roles, and maybe the adult role players will be supplemented by costumed children playing freely in the way children of the period might have. As a part of the larger scene, you'll have to know how all the parts fit together.

Visitors will want to know how all these people tending shops, baking pies, and weaving rugs actually make a living. Where does the housewife get the money to spend on flour for the pie, and on hoops and marbles for the children? What is the source of money for the merchant and weaver? The answers, of course, lie in the town's original reason for existence. If it was an agricultural trading center, you'd better know that the factor's warehouse is even more important than the local tavern, and the nature of the area's export crop. If the town was supported by an industry of some sort, then you ought to be conversant with its function and impact.

The Living Military Post If you're assigned to work at a military post where living history is the method of interpretation, you have a lot of drilling and studying to do. You'll be learning a whole new social structure. You'll learn the importance of the commander's headquarters, the place from which came orders directing every phase of life, including what time garrison wives could hang out their laundry, and by what time children's toys have to be taken in from the quarters' yards. You'll need to know what quirks were peculiar to the commander of your post. You'll come to realize with whom you can fraternize and with whom you can't. If you're an enlisted man, you'll discover your unloved and unwanted status.

If you're to play the role of a soldier's wife, you'll become aware of the rigid caste system, all about the officer's wife who is trying to maintain at least the appearance of upper class life without getting her husband cashiered for debt; the sergeant's wife who is struggling to make a decent home on inadequate pay; and down on Soapsuds Row, the private's wife, who is being tolerated on the post only as a laundress. What does a soldier's wife do all day while her husband is away? How are the children educated? What games do they play? Do the women have social organizations? What birthing methods are used?

As you can see, there's much to learn. As you're learning, remember the key words: valid, accurate, and indepth.

The Living Farm At the time of the American Revolution, about 90 percent of the population was rural compared with about 8 percent today. This indicates a major change in agricultural processes. These changes are sometimes demonstrated at various park sites using the living history mode. If you're assigned to one of these places, you'll be learning a whole new technology, or, more accurately, unlearning the one you presently know. You'll become acquainted with reproductions of antique tools, new ways of looking at the soil. You'll be going through old wills, census records, diaries, letters, newspapers, catalogues, etc., in an attempt to discover what farming was like in the period you're portraying. You'll find that you'll have to do a lot of compromising with the reality of your period. It'll be difficult to find unhybridized seed and animals, and the matter of disease and pest control will cause you problems as well. Tubercular cows may have been common in a bygone century, but they would hardly be allowed now, nor would it be acceptable to expose neighboring farmers to pests from your infested fields in order to preserve an historic scene.

Safety will require further compromise. Farm machinery can be very dangerous, and few visitors would appreciate being butted by a fractious goat. So, more fencing than would have been necessary in an earlier period may have to be installed.

Even with all of these compromises, there's still plenty of opportunity for you to share with visitors the agricultural scene from another time.

Environmental Living This is a role-playing event which has been primarily conducted for school children, although there's no reason to so limit it. Basically, children play the roles of those who used to live at historic sites. If you're assigned to one of the several historic sites which has this program, you'll first work with teachers in a workshop on the site, explaining the program and allowing them to try the role playing themselves. At this first session, you'll give the teachers bibliographies and other materials which will help them prepare the children to visit the site to play their roles. Then, you'll be at the school interpreting the site. The third step in the process is an overnight visit to the site by the children where they eat, sleep, work, and play as the earlier inhabitants did. Finally, you visit the children again at their school after their overnight visit to discuss the relevancy of their experience.

If you're involved with this kind of activity, you can have a real impact on the children's learning. You can help them to know how to do historical research, to realize that history is made up of events in the lives of people at all levels of society, to make a meaningful contrast between life in the past and present. They may begin to see that life without the relatively abundant energy of our era took a lot of human energy. You can raise questions as to what's happened to the environment since the time in which their role playing took place, and ask what they think the future portends. You can often use this program to acquaint the children with other cultures, to point out the values of diversity.

DEMONSTRATIONS IN NATURAL AREAS

Before reading this section, it may be helpful to review the general comments on demonstrations on pages 79–80. Natural area demonstrations are future-oriented, while historical demonstrations explain the past. Demonstrations of such things as backpacking, fly fishing, maps and compass use, swimming, mulepacking, snorkeling, kite flying, frisbie throwing, all imply the explanation of a process with the idea in mind that visitors will probably use this instructional information at some later time. This makes a difference as to the way the demonstration is approached. If you're giving such a demonstration, the process will need to be slower, more deliberate. You should give more opportunity to ask questions so as to clear up the more obscure parts of the process. "Hands on" experience by each of the participants is often desirable, and this can only be accomplished if the size of your audience is restricted. There will be more need for feedback than in the historical demonstration. You will need to provide ample time to check the continuing progress in visitor understanding. Periodic summaries of what you've covered up to that moment will be helpful.

In natural area demonstrations, as in historical demon-

strations, it's important to use the process as an "excuse" to interpret the bigger concepts. The purpose of giving a backpacking demonstration is not just to make it easier for visitors, but also to give them an appreciation for the area, an understanding of the rules and regulations, so as to provide for their safety and the protection of the area.

Not all natural area demonstrations need be "useful." A recent role-playing demonstration at Yellowstone's Old Faithful had park visitors playing the roles of magma, water molecules, steam bubbles, and the molecules of silica which line the geyser's plumbing. As the magma heated the water molecules, steam bubbles appeared and began to agitate the cap of colder water molecules at the top of the geyser's plumbing. The agitation finally became so great that all of the visitors playing water molecules and steam bubbles were allowed to escape in an exploding fashion past the visitors playing the silica molecules.

SKY INTERPRETATION

Interpretation of the sky is one of the more recent entries in the interpretive repertoire of most natural area parks. Some may still raise the question: "Why interpret the sky?" The most obvious answer is: "Because it's there." The sky is within the boundaries of any park. Even if we only interpreted the brightest star in the sky, our sun, in relation to the earth's surface, that would be a significant thing to do. Then, when the sun is related to our weather, which can be thought of as coming from the sky, and the weather is related to nearly all the growing things on the earth, the significance of sky interpretation becomes even more important.

There are other reasons for sky interpretation. (1) It can help give us a geological understanding of the earth's origin. (2) It sharply distinguishes the difference between a natural and city sky. (3) Since the earth is a part of the universe, sky interpretation helps us understand our place within that context. (4) It can help us appreciate the life support system on spaceship earth and to realize how vulnerable it is. (5) It can help us question who we are as human beings, and encourage us to re-examine our value systems. (6) It can give us insight to earlier peoples for whom the sky had great meanings.

If you're going to be doing sky interpretation, it would seem important to develop one or more of the big ideas listed above. Too often sky interpretation is merely a process of locating this star or that constellation with a few facts thrown in. This is usually very dull because there is no attempt to make the sky relevant to the lives of the people in the audience, or to the site where the talk is being given.

[For a review of this chapter, see questions 61 through 90 in Chapter 8.]

Chapter 6

Walks, Tours and Hikes

GENERAL   Most of what you'll need to know to lead an effective walk, tour or hike is included under "Primary Elements of Interpretation," pp. 32-55. It's suggested that you review that section before proceeding with this one.

In this section, some of the unique characteristics of giving walks, tours, and hikes will be highlighted. (Although the following definitions may be somewhat arbitrary, they indicate what I mean when I use these terms.) A **walk** is usually a natural area activity involving walking for up to about three hours. A **tour** is the same as a walk except that it takes place in an historic setting. A **hike** is an extended walk lasting one-half day or more. Each of these activities gives you an opportunity to provide a personalized service. You don't have to be anyone but yourself, you have less structure than a talk requires, you'll be less pressured than at the visitor center information desk, and you'll be in the midst of what you're talking about instead of having to rely on slides, models, objects, and word pictures. Because there's less structure, you can more easily adapt to the unique character of the group you're leading. Aren't you fortunate to have so much in your favor?

When conducting groups, you'll have two major concerns: (1) moving people from place to place, and (2) providing interpretation along the way. The first concern is more unique to walks, tours, and hikes than the second and will, therefore, receive more attention.

MOVING PEOPLE FROM PLACE TO PLACE

Before the walk, tour, or hike begins It's a good idea to be at the assembly point at least fifteen minutes before the time scheduled for your activity to begin. Your uniform or costume immediately identifies you as the person who will be conducting the activity. This allows you to take the initiative and approach those who have assembled with enthusiasm and a spirit of friendliness. Your purpose is to let people know that something is about to start, that it promises to be an interesting event, that you're going to handle it, that you're a capable and friendly sort of person to be with on such an occasion. Show the people that you'll be talking *with* them, not *to* them. The attitudes you establish at the beginning will help you maintain that desirable conversational approach even though the group becomes too large for actual conversation. Avoid being dominated by individuals, but circulate; let as many people as possible interact with you.

This will be your opportunity, too, to size up the group. What are their interests? What do they expect from this activity? Are they familiar with this area? How much background information will they need?

Start on Time When the starting time arrives, begin at once. Don't make those who were on time "wait a few more minutes" for latecomers. Take charge in a positive manner. The people expect you to be a leader, and a listless, uncertain, delayed beginning will weaken your credibility. Greet them as a group, introduce yourself, and, if you wish, tell them something about you. Identify yourself as a member of the National Park Service. When the group isn't too large, you might ask the members to introduce themselves and tell where they're from.

Tell the group where you're going, what you'll be doing along the way, and when you'll be back. Mention, but don't over-emphasize, any difficulties that may be encountered, such as slippery surfaces, steep inclines, and narrow passageways. Invite everyone to go with you.

If there are special rules and regulations to be observed during the activity, now's the time to mention them in a positive way. If you don't state them at the beginning, visitors will have good reason for being offended when you later reprimand them, no matter how gently you do it. Explain why the special considerations are necessary. Now's a good time to ask family groups to stay together. This will provide a greater amount of safety, and will help prevent a pack of children from tripping over your heels to be closest to you.

After a brief introduction, move the group to a second location, even though it isn't far away, to let them know this isn't going to be a static activity. Show and discuss something that will vividly support the theme you've chosen. Remember to involve the group, use questions, and, in general, use the principles of interpretation explained earlier.

Your Progress Along the Way Small groups present fewer problems of movement. If you talk *with* rather than *to* your group, if your leadership is exercised unobtrusively, and if you're sensitive to your group, their responses will indicate how fast to move, when to stop, how long to talk, and even what to say. Establish good rapport, and a small group will almost run itself.

As group size increases, your problems of movement

multiply. Large groups require more time for starting, moving, reassembling, and unless expertly handled, movement can rob you of time for interpretation. Set a pace that's not tiring, and at the same time, not slow enough to be boring. When your group isn't too large, make frequent stops, but make them short. Frequent moves give the activity a sense of action, of something going on, and more short stops provide rest intervals. For larger groups, stops must be fewer, but should not be prolonged merely to enable you to tell the whole story. Shorten the material you cover, rather than prolong the stops.

When you wish to assemble a group of people for a stop, walk to the point where you want the furthest edge of the audience to be, stop the group and then walk back to the middle. If you stop at the middle and ask the group to go on to where you want the edge to be, it'll be much more complicated and confusing.

Have a definite point for dismissal, and let the group know the activity is over. Don't let it just disintegrate. When you're at some distance from the starting point, describe those things that are available to those who would explore further, and invite the rest to walk back with you to the point of origin. On a loop trip, where you return to where you started, stop for the interpretive climax before the group sees the destination and becomes restless.

Some General Suggestions Keep in the lead at all times, and talk to all of the group. Keep those at the rear in view and in mind. Make sure they can see and hear.

As you move from place to place, converse with those near you if you wish, but make it obvious that no one is missing anything important. Repeat the important observations, and repeat the questions that were asked so that

everyone knows what's going on. Talking to the entire group while you're walking isn't a good idea unless the group is very small. If you stand in what seems like a hazardous place while you're interacting with the group, some people will be so concerned for your safety that they won't hear a word you say.

PROVIDING INTERPRETATION
ALONG THE WAY

Although themes, outlines, etc., are just as important for this activity as any other, there is more room for flexibility in your interpretation as you adapt to a changing scene and to different groups. A conducted walk, tour, or hike is always evolving, and you'll probably do the activity several times before you feel comfortable with it. Hopefully, you'll never become completely satisfied, but you'll keep looking for ways to make it better, to vary it. Nothing is as deadly as a canned spiel in any interpretive activity. Avoid doing the activity in exactly the same way each time you do it.

GUIDED TOURS OF HISTORICAL AREAS

Historical areas tend to fall into three categories: (1) places where nationally significant historical events have taken place, (2) places where an important person was once involved, and (3) places which represent or memorialize major themes of American history, such as national expansion, economic growth, industrialism, agricultural development, freedom and personal opportunity, cultural growth. The Statue of Liberty National Monument, Hopewell Village National Historic Site, and Jefferson National Expansion Memorial National Historic Site are examples of the latter category.

The primary value of categorizing areas is to help determine relevant interpretation. If the place you're interpreting is one where an important *event* took place, then the emphasis should be on the importance of that event in history, and its relevancy to today's visitor. Interpretation of the Golden Spike National Historic Site, for example, would be relevant only if it brought that event to life and showed its significance in the expansion of America, especially its economic and social growth. Similarly, interpretation at the Carl Sandburg Home National Historic Site, or the Clara Barton National Historic Site will be relevant only if emphasis is placed on the lives of these people and their importance to the world today.

Once relevance has been decided, themes can be determined and developed. Some possible themes are:

(1) Several forces working together made it possible for the nation to be joined at Golden Spike.

(2) Clara Barton's humanitarian activities during the Civil War led to the establishment of the American Red Cross.

(3) Carl Sandburg was important as an interpreter of

American life and legend.

(4) The Statue of Liberty symbolizes the lure of America to immigrants as a land of greater freedom and opportunity.

Once you've selected a theme and decided how you're going to develop it, you'll need to consider several problems unique to historical areas. One of the biggest problems derives from the *static* nature of the site you'll be interpreting. Keeping historical tours alive is a problem because the thing that made your area important has come and gone. Only the reminder of what once happened remains. Now, it's up to you to bring the area back to life. You can activate the imaginations of your visitors by humanizing the area, that is, by putting people into the scene, and by picturing the scene as it was historically. History becomes interesting most often when its human aspects are emphasized, and the more specific you can be about the people who were once involved in your site's history, the more effective you'll be. Reading excerpts from diaries, letters and poetry they wrote; singing songs they used to sing or listen to; describing a meal they might have eaten; revealing the concern they had for political and social issues; portraying their energy situation; discussing familial relationships; showing blowups of old photos, prints and artwork; are just a few examples of how you can humanize your area and spark the kind of imaginative interest that's carried back home.

How many times can you take people on the same tour without getting bored with it, without doing it by rote, without sounding like a tape recorder? A "canned" approach can be best avoided by realizing that although the area itself doesn't change in any significant way, there are three things which do change that you can capitalize on: (1) yourself, (2) your knowledge of the area, and (3) the audience. By constantly learning more about your area, you'll have more and more material to choose from for your presentation. You'll discover new approaches, other points of view, more in-depth material about those who once peopled the area. As you change, you can keep refreshing your presentation. Audiences change, too. By involving your audience, by finding out who they are, what they want to know, you can adapt your presentation to the uniqueness of each audience. As you search for relevancy for your presentation, you can keep up with current issues which hold the public's interest so you can more adequately compare the past and present to give visitors the benefit of the insight of the past on today's problems.

You can help make your area come alive if you show exact spots where things happened and let people have the experience of standing there. There's something special about standing exactly where Alexander Hamilton, Theodore Roosevelt, Martha Washington, and others have stood.

It will be important to put the events you're describing into a context. What else was happening in the world at the same time, among similar people? How did the geography of the area, for instance, affect what happened?

Who are the people who come to historical areas and participate in interpretive activities? Are they different from those who visit natural areas? Unfortunately, not much is known about this important subject, but from what has been observed, it seems safe to assume that:

• Most visitors have only a superficial knowledge of history, and will need considerable background material before they'll be able to appreciate your area.

• Most visitors have a great interest and curiosity

about the people who were part of the events occurring at the place they're visiting. They'll want to know about prisoners if they're at Alcatraz, the immigrants at Ellis Island, factory workers at Saugus Iron Works. What did they wear, eat; what did they do for entertainment; what were their morals, values, and customs; what did they read; how much and by what means did they travel, etc.?

• Most visitors will have visited one or more other historic areas, and they'll want to know what makes you special to them.

• Most visitors, being more interested in people than in things, will be bored by mere identification of objects or too many facts and dates.

• Most visitors aren't interested in knowing who donated what.

• Most visitors will be turned off if your presentation is in bad taste, if you're cheap, sensational and vulgar. You must avoid the temptation to exaggerate for effect.

• Most visitors won't be interested in your personal opinions on controversial matters.

• Most visitors won't want to hear all you know. Be selective.

• Most visitors will want you to adapt your presentation to them.

An excellent reference which is highly recommended for interpreters of historic sites is *Interpretation of Historic Sites* by William T. Alderson and Shirley Payne Low (Nashville: American Association for State and Local History, 1976).

The Historic Structure The space in an historic structure is often limited. This makes it necessary to schedule tours in such a way that they don't overlap with each other. Sometimes, space is such a problem that guided

tours are impossible, and the "stationing" technique must be used. That is, people are stationed at various places within the structure to interpret that particular location to people as they walk through on their own. If you're stationed in an historic structure, the suggestions given under roving interpretation (p. 64) may be helpful.

In the peak of the season, people may have to wait quite a while before it will be possible for them to tour the structure. Spend as much time as possible with the group before the tour begins. This will probably help time pass more quickly and enjoyably. Even though you'll be pushed to move the group with dispatch, so as not to hold up following groups, avoid conveying this pressure to visitors. One way you can do this is to not make reference to other groups, especially the one just in front of you or the one following behind. Avoid expressions such as: "Well, it's time we were on our way," or "My watch tells me that . . ." or "If we're going to be through on time, we'd better be moving on." Make the experience a relaxing one for the visitor. Use expressions such as "Now that we've discovered this principle, let's see how it applies at . . ." or "On our way to_____,you might be thinking about . . ."

As you move from place to place within the structure, help the visitor to create images of what happened there. Help them visualize people doing things. If it's the bedroom of an historic home, you can help the visitor imagine one of the occupants at the foot of the bed tightening the ropes that served in that period as bedsprings. You could call attention to the short length of the bed piled high with pillows, and help visitors visualize occupants sleeping while propped up. "Why did they sleep that way?" you could ask, even if only rhetorically. "Because they thought that sleeping in a propped-up position prevented consumption," you could reply.

Or, suppose you're in the drawing room. Your explanation of how that space came to be called "drawing room" could lead to a discussion of the status of women in earlier times. You could describe how, after the meal had been served at a social gathering, the women went to the "withdrawing" room (later shortened to drawing room) so the men wouldn't be hampered in their discussion of "serious matters."

Returning to the bedroom, you could call attention to the fact that the bed is at a much higher level than in homes today, and help the audience understand that the higher a bed is in a room, the warmer it will be. The high bed also leaves room under it for a trundle bed.

Or, suppose you're in the bakery at Fort Vancouver. You could help the visitor smell the various breads and pastries being baked and imagine the more primitive processes of baking used in an earlier day.

You're at the spring near Fort Clatsop where Lewis and Clark drew their water. You walk your group over the trail they used, helping them imagine what it would be like to carry water over that terrain in winter.

Special attention needs to be given to children on tours

through historic structures. If the structure is a home, what did the children do there? What playthings did they have? What was their status at the dinner table? How were they educated? Were equal freedoms given to both sexes?

Involve the group in the scene as much as possible. Ask questions such as: "If you were coming to this home for dinner, what would you be expected to wear? What time of day would you be coming? What behavior would have been expected of the women guests, the men guests? What subjects, if any, should you avoid discussing? Should you limit your conversation to only those on either side of you? What food would you likely be served? How were you allowed to eat it? What smells would be apparent? How would the lack of air-conditioning or central heating affect the situation? Would you play games after dinner? What kind?"

Share yourself with the group. If you've had experiences with previous groups on this tour that would shed some light, or provide some amusement to this situation (as long as it doesn't make fun of earlier visitors) it would be appropriate to share it.

Invite others to share themselves with you. You may learn quite a few new things by assuming that you don't know everything, and that some visitors may have special knowledge that would interest you and others.

A final thought. Since the area you're taking people through is irreplaceable in its original form, great care must be taken to make sure that visitors understand what they may touch, where they may sit, and where they should do neither of these things. All restrictions necessary for the preservation of the site should be carefully explained at the beginning of the tour. Be sure visitors understand why these restrictions are necessary.

The Battlefield There are many ways of looking at yesterday's battlefields. Today, they are calm, serene and often beautiful with well-kept lawns, shrubbery, flowers, and trees. A battle, however, is anything but pretty, and it will be up to you as an interpreter to bring back the stench, confusion, gore, shrieks of wounded and dying men, the ear-splitting sounds of exploding guns and artillery. *Accuracy* is of the utmost importance as war is interpreted. The glorification of war is a disservice to the human race.

As you lead tours over battlefields, it will be important for you to help visitors visualize what happened at this location that made it important enough to be designated a national historic site. Not only should you give the big, overall picture, including the relationship of this battle to other battles, but you should also "humanize" the interpretation by helping us know some of the individuals who were involved in the situation. These individuals would include the recruit as well as the officer, relatives and loved ones at home, inhabitants at or near the battlefield.

Look for vantage points on the battlefield, like elevated sites, from which you can point to physical remains and places that help fill in the picture. Much of what was originally there will be gone and you'll have to recreate it in the visitors' minds. Give a careful geographic orientation with reference to locations with which the visitor might be familiar, like Washington, D. C., is so many miles in that direction, or Richmond lies so many miles over there. Sometimes, it's important to point out which way north is, especially at Gettysburg where, curiously enough, the initial Confederate troops came in from the north. Where hills, mountains, rivers, or other geographical locations are important to our understanding of what happened on this battlefield, they should be pointed out.

You probably should not try to tell the whole story during the tour, but suggest that various displays, publications and/or movies at the visitor center, or in other buildings, will help fill in the story you're telling on the tour.

A balanced account of the battle should be provided. Avoid giving the impression that you think one "side" was "better" than the other. It should also be realized that much of the interpretation of any battlefield is controversial. Raise the question as to whether the battle was necessary. You must become familiar with the controversies, and present them as unresolved matters if, indeed, they are unresolved, as most of them are. As more facts become available, some controversies will be laid to rest, but new ones will arise. You should always be searching for new information and interpretations.

The Archaeological Site Interpretive tours at archaeological sites differ in two major ways from other historical tours. These differences are more a matter of degree than substance. First, because of their greater antiquity, they tend to be more fragile, more easily damaged, vandalized. Thus it will be important for you, if you're going to be interpreting at an archaeological site, to help people understand why collecting artifacts is not allowed. Collecting is not allowed in any park area (natural or historic), of course, without a permit, but the problem is generally worse at archaeological sites because an artifact's significance can only be adequately understood within the context of where it was found. Searching for artifacts is something like reading a book, except that in archaeology, you have to tear out each page as you read it. Archaeologists read and record what

was on each page so it isn't lost, whereas the average collector can't read the page (understand the significance of what's been found) and doesn't bother to record it. The page plucked from the earth by the average collector is gone. Even if the artifact is recovered, it's relatively useless out of its original location.

In 1906, Congress passed An Act for the Preservation of American Antiquities which prohibits the appropriation, excavation, injury or destruction of any object of antiquity situated on federal lands. It also gave the president authority to set aside areas called national monuments on public land to preserve prehistoric structures, historic structures, objects, landmarks and objects of scientific interest.

Subsequent legislation has strengthened the protection of prehistoric and historic sites. As an interpreter at one of these sites, you can do much to help the public understand the reasons behind protective legislation.

The second major difference stems from the much greater amount of time separating your period of time from the age you'll be interpreting. This means it'll be more difficult to draw parallels between then and now. And, of course, you'll know a lot less about those who peopled these areas because the records of their existence aren't as abundant as for more recent times. You'll probably have to be even more careful in what you assert and how you assert it.

Even though you'll know less about people of antiquity, you'll find that visitors have a great curiosity about ancient people, and that will present you with the fascinating challenge of putting together the pieces of an exciting puzzle.

GUIDED WALKS AND HIKES IN NATURAL AREAS

You've inventoried the trail, and from your long list of what you *could* talk about, you've narrowed your subject to a workable theme. You've decided on your main headings and subheadings and chosen support material that'll make your theme an exciting idea. You've reviewed the primary elements of interpretation and the suggestions for walks, tours and hikes in general. You're about ready to go, but before you do, you may want to consider a few additional suggestions about specific kinds of activities.

The Short Walk Even though you'll only be gone a relatively short time, make sure everyone knows what will be expected of them. Check to see if they're properly dressed and otherwise equipped for the activity.

As you move from point to point, practice conservation. Pick up a scrap of paper or other litter occasionally and dispose of it properly. It won't be necessary to explain—your purpose will be obvious.

Checklists of birds and animals are useful aids to take with you on walks, as are guidebooks to flowers, geology, animal tracks, etc. Hand lenses, thermometers, maps and other such devices are handy to include in your pack.

If your group meets a horseback party, yield the right-of-way. Take your group off to one side of the trail so the horses won't have to pass between walls of people. Caution your group to stand quietly until the horses have passed.

If circumstances prevent your return at the announced time, let the group know soon enough so that any who have schedules to meet can return ahead of the rest.

Where there's any unusual element of danger, particularly that of getting lost, keep close check of the group, counting noses from time to time. Ask people to let you know if they leave the group. Say what needs to be said about snakes, poison ivy, bears and other potential dangers early in the activity, but avoid overdoing it.

If there's an accident, you have two responsibilities, to your group and to the injured person. If available in your area, take along a portable radio transmitter to report accidents and to seek help.

Although your attention will be diverted to the injured person, you'll still have a responsibility to your group, to make sure that they return safely to the beginning of the trail. Sometimes your group may be released to return on its own. Explain the situation and get approval of the group before releasing them. If there's any possibility of them losing the way, keep the group together, perhaps under the leadership of an experienced volunteer whom the group agrees to accept. Sometimes you may have to take them back yourself, leaving capable volunteers with the injured, and in very exceptional cases, you may find it necessary to hold everyone until relief comes to the scene.

You can better aid the injured person if you ask your group to wait for you *away from the scene of the accident*. Secure a volunteer to assist you, evaluate the situation, and give first aid. Determine whether or not the injured person can be moved, or whether s/he should remain until additional help arrives. Ideally, there won't be any accidents, and anything you can do to prevent them is far better than giving first aid afterwards.

As you proceed with your group on a walk, let people *experience* nature rather than be told about it all the time. Find a place where all the senses can be used, invite your group to be seated, and suggest that no one talk (including yourself) for several minutes. The group may appreciate a rest from your voice, and an opportunity to savor that particular place.

Remember, too, to keep involving the group in the interpretive process. Ask the members of your group to be looking for things they can share with the other visitors. Explain that you alone can't possibly see all there is that's worth talking about. Maybe someone else will spot the squirrel, or moose, or calypso orchid that you would have missed.

I used to lead a short walk of about 3 hours through Yellowstone's Pocket Basin, and I'd like to share with you some of the things I did to involve my groups.

There was one place in the basin that had a very unusual odor. As we approached this particular area, I'd ask the group to be aware of this odor, and to try to figure out what it smelled like, what it reminded them of. As we'd cross the area, the smell would become obvious to most of the group, and they'd report that it smelled "sweet" or "syrupy" or "burned." Then, I'd encourage the group to try to figure out the origin and cause of the smell. We'd look around and see that there were lots of lodgepole pines with red needles on them, indicating they were dying, and we'd see bare patches of ground where there was no vegetation at all. I'd ask "What do you sup-

pose killed the trees? Do you think there's any relationship between the smell and the fact that the trees are dying and the the ground vegetation is dead?"

Then I'd tell them something they couldn't observe. "This sweet, syrupy odor has been here only since 1959. Does that help any?" Some of the people in the group would remember that Yellowstone had a major earthquake in 1959, and that the quake caused a lot of changes in the geysers and hot springs. It was then possible to explain: "The earthquake opened up new cracks and fissures in the earth's crust where we're standing, allowing steam to come up through the earth to the roots of these trees and other plants. It's steam from molten rock below us that's cooking the roots of the vegetation in the area that's causing the sweet, burned odor."

As a final step in the involvement process, I'd take the group over to the dead and dying trees and say: "I want you to know that it really is steam heat that's killing these trees." I'd dig a little bit of the earth away from the roots and invite each member of the group to put a hand into the opening to actually feel the heat. That's a sensation

everyone seemed to enjoy, and one which was probably memorable.

As you show people things along a trail, look for those things which will cause people to say to themselves, "I didn't know that!" One such thing might be a mass of ladybugs on a cold day. You could explain that ladybugs survive cold weather by massing together. Those on the outside of the mass squirm to the inside for warmth only to be eventually replaced by another "outsider." Honeybees and cluster flies huddle together in the same way.

Pay special attention to children on walks—they're people too. Give them something to do that they'll remember. You could have one of them shake hands with a spruce tree and report to the group what it felt like. Another could stand at the side of a trail pointing out something you'd explained in advance. A third child could be given the responsibility of counting the people in the group. A fourth could pass among the group showing a specimen too small to be seen at a distance. And so on.

The Extended Hike The suggestions given for the short

walk are, of course, applicable here. Here are some additional ideas.

After carefully checking topographic maps, choose several possible areas and then narrow the choice by asking such questions as: (1) Can the distance be covered in the time available? (2) Is there adequate parking at the trailhead? (3) Is the topography, especially elevation changes, too difficult for the group I'm likely to attract? (4) What special conditions will I face such as late snow cover, wet conditions, stream crossings, insects, water supply, camping areas, dangerous plants and animals, lightning strikes, accessibility for emergency medical problems? (5) Does the area have enough variety to maintain interest for an extended time? (6) Can this hike be given in this area without causing unacceptable damage to the resource? (7) Am I prepared to handle emergency backcountry problems that might develop such as: (a) medical problems (cardiac arrest, burns, broken bones, bleeding, etc.), (b) off-trail travel with compass and map (to avoid a fire, etc.), (c) encounters with wild animals, (d) severe changes in the weather, (e) lost party members.

Do a "dry run" of the hike with some people who are in "average to below average" physical condition to check out the area for interpretive possibilities, safety considerations, camping areas, rest stops, etc. Determine the equipment both you and the visitors will need. Ask yourself some key questions: (1) Am I secure enough in my interpretive abilities to hold the interest of my group for an extended time? (2) Am I sufficiently experienced in "outdoors ability" to gain the confidence and respect of my group? (3) Do I know enough about group behavior to bring out the potential in nearly any group?

The longer the hike, the more carefully you'll have to

check to make sure each person knows just how difficult the trip is. Before leaving, assure yourself that everyone is adequately clothed, equipped and physically capable. Although it's very difficult to measure physical capability, you'll have to make the best judgment you can. Usually, people will understand when you carefully explain to them why they should *not* go on the hike, but if you have to, politely refuse to let the unprepared accompany you.

Set a pace adjusted to the abilities of the group and the difficulties of the terrain. Frequent short rests generally work better than longer rests at less frequent intervals. Use rest stops as interpretive opportunities.

Count your group soon after you're underway, and count them again at strategic places along the way. You should always know where the members of your group are.

Suppose you're half way to your destination, and someone wants to go back. This possibility should have been discussed at the beginning of the hike and an understanding agreed to, but unless it's dangerous for someone to leave you and return, don't over-encourage continuation. If you're coming back the same way, you might suggest that the person wait until you return, or that s/he continue behind you at a more leisurely pace—if the trail is clear and the person agrees not to leave the trail. If the person insists on going back, describe exactly how to return, instruct him/her not to leave the trail, and try to find someone else who would like to go back with him/her.

Avoid dangerous situations. Don't urge people to an experience which, while perfectly safe in your opinion, is new and appears dangerous to them. Nor should you over-dramatize such situations. Approach stairways, ladders, narrow or steep trails casually. Say what needs to be said, pass on, and lend a hand to those who seem to need it.

Carry first-aid materials, and know how to use them. You should have a Red Cross first-aid card, or its equivalent, if you're going to be leading hikes.

If the line spreads out too far behind you, perhaps you're moving too fast, or not stopping often enough.

If there are no restroom facilities along the way, the group should be told that at the beginning of the hike. Some hike leaders prefer to let people drop out for a few minutes, when the need arises, and then catch up with the group on their own. Others take all the men up the trail, telling the women to wait five minutes, and then follow. Which method is better for you depends on the terrain and the clarity of the trail. Instruction should be given early in the hike about proper disposal of human feces in wilderness areas.

Children under 14 are welcome on extended hikes only

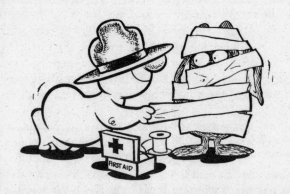

if they're accompanied by an adult responsible for their behavior and safety.

If you're leading an overnight hike, you'll especially want to make sure that everyone has adequate food, water, and shelter, but you should take no responsibility for the cooking, packing, and putting up of shelters. The group should know in advance whether pit fires will be used, or if they'll need to bring their own stoves. They'll also need to know if there's potable water along the way.

The overnight hike is an ideal situation to help people understand the relationship between people and their environment. Care should be taken to have a minimum impact on your immediate environment. Ideally, an overnight hike will be preceded by a backpacking demonstration, and if reservations are required for the event, as they often are, instructions can be given to participants well in advance of the activity itself.

OTHER MODES OF TRANSPORTATION

In these days of dwindling fossil fuel supplies, it's probably better to encourage non-fuel-consumptive activities, but there are some areas difficult to get to without motorized transport.

Water Transportation

Tour Boats Typical of the areas it would be difficult to get to without motorized transport is Glacier Bay in Alaska. It'd be unsafe for most people to see this area by hand-propelled craft although John Muir and others have done it. If a tour boat were not available, people would probably hire individual motor boats. Public transportation on a fully loaded large boat probably uses less fuel than many small boats. It also enables an interpreter to reach more people at the same time. So the tour boat can be an appropriate tool of interpretation on large bodies of water.

On most tour boats you'll have a captive audience. If they want to escape your interpretation, it'll be difficult without earplugs. (Maybe you should supply some.) This means that you'll need to be extra-sensitive to the needs of your group. Many of the people on a tour boat will want to just appreciate the majesty of the scenery without knowing all about its geological origin. Plan some silent times in your presentation.

If the tour is a long one, visit informally with small groups on the boat rather than presenting all of your message to everyone. Let the group tell you what they want by encouraging lots of questions. Avoid the temptation to amuse the group with jokes and irrelevant stories.

It would probably be helpful to introduce the tour at the boat dock so people will know what to expect, what to look for. Once the boat is in motion, it's advisable to start talking about a given feature before it comes into prominence, and get to the climax just as it comes into the best view.

Canoes Leading a number of canoes into a natural area can be a very rewarding experience. This means of transportation is silent, historic, uses no fossil energy, and doesn't even leave footprints.

Safety will be your chief concern on a canoe trip, and related to that will be the necessity, probably, to give some basic instruction in canoe handling. For some people, it will be a first-time experience, while for others, it will be "old hat." Perhaps you can persuade the more experienced canoeists to help you instruct the neophytes.

Tell the group what to expect before you begin the trip, but be prepared for the unexpected as a waterway is a very non-static place. As you move along, tell the group what's up ahead so they can be prepared to see it before they've passed by it.

The group probably won't want to be in their canoes all the time, so plan some ashore as well as afloat activities. When there's something special to see, gather the canoes around yours, and make sure it's visible to everyone.

Since weather will be a big factor, chart out emergency landing sites. Make sure everyone is wearing a life preserver and observing other safety rules.

Motorized Vehicles

Auto Caravans Auto caravans can cause such major traffic problems that one must seriously consider their viability as a means of interpretation. In park areas where there is an off-season, when traffic is light, caravans can be used effectively. If the planned trip is a loop, suggest carpooling to reduce congestion, pollution and fuel use. Carpooling may also encourage the development of new friendships.

One of the most recently used techniques for caravans involves the use of citizen band radio. Each car in the caravan is given a receiver that will pick up the frequency used on the citizen band transmitter in the lead car. In this way, the interpreter in the lead car can talk to those in the caravan as the cars are moving and describe whatever is visible to all the cars. Even when the caravan comes to a stop, this method makes it largely unnecessary for everyone to pile out of their cars and assemble at a central point to receive a message.

If you're giving the message from the lead car, you'll want to have a theme for the event, and follow all of the pertinent primary elements of interpretation discussed earlier. At the same time, you should take advantage of spontaneous happenings which occur as you move along. One of the handicaps of this kind of interpretation is the lack of immediate feedback. You can compensate for this, to some extent, by assembling the group as a whole, now and then, to find out what questions they have.

Trams Trams loaded with park visitors are pulled behind pickup trucks and other vehicles in some park

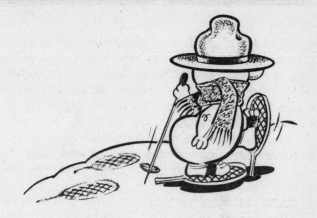

areas. Their chief advantage is that they concentrate the visitors in one place and, by using mass transit, make traffic problems like parking cars and cars being bumper-to-bumper non-existent.

If you're leading a tram group, you should make a special effort to make yourself visible to those on the tram. This will often mean stopping the trams, and getting off to the side of the road where all can see you. In this way you can get feedback from the group, and they will have an opportunity to ask you questions.

Winter Considerations

Winter means one thing to low-elevation southern parks, another to low-lying coastal areas, and still something else to high-elevation and northern park areas where most roads are closed by heavy snows. While the "mechanics" of interpretation don't change much in areas outside the snowbelt, they change considerably at the snowed-in areas.

How do you provide interpretation to people on snowmachines who are reasonably more concerned with their own survival in -40° F weather than knowing that frogs develop a sort of anti-freeze to assure their winter survival? There are lots of ways to enjoy a park area, and as long as this enjoyment doesn't damage the environment, who's to say that one way is better than another? Maybe it's legitimate to enjoy a park without having information loaded onto the situation . . . or maybe it's just a different kind of interpretation. Maybe empathetic listening to a winter visitor in a warming hut, and celebrating with that person his/her survival over adverse weather conditions is enough.

Maybe the visitor has seen a marvelous display of animal life, and telling you about it intensifies the original experience. It would appear that it's important for winter interpreters to be especially good listeners.

On the other hand, visitors who come to snow-bound parks have made a lot of effort to be there, and thus may be even more highly motivated to learn in depth about the park than summer visitors who are trying to do three parks in one day. They may be in your local area for two or three days, and take one or more snowshoe or ski touring trips with you.

Up to 90% of those who'll be going with you on snowshoes and skis will be trying out these devices for the first time. This means that (1) you'll have to give at least some instruction in the use of the equipment before you begin traveling, (2) you won't be able to cover great distances, although you'll probably find that even novices will be able to move faster on skis than they do on foot, and (3) you'll have to be especially safety conscious. Visitors should be told that because most of them are novices, they should expect to occasionally fall down. Most of the time this will add to the merriment of the situation, but if a person gets too wet and a cold wind is blowing, watch out for hypothermia, and know how to cope with this loss of body heat.

Since park scenery and wildlife displays are especially spectacular in the winter, and because it's more difficult to gather groups on snowshoes and skis, perhaps greater reliance should be placed on the resource as a source of inspiration than as a learning laboratory.

Interpreters in snowbound parks lead a very isolated existence as there is no outside entertainment. If you're to be a winter interpreter, you'll need to be a person who is comfortable with himself/herself and just a few others.

[For a review of this chapter, see questions 91 through 149 in Chapter 8.]

Chapter 7

Special Considerations

Nearly everything you'll need to know, as you begin the process of being an interpreter, has been covered, but there are a few additional items for you to consider.

RECREATION AREAS

Originally, national recreation areas were places around reservoirs which lay behind dams built by agencies other than the National Park Service. Typical of these would be Lake Mead National Recreation Area which was the first such area to be established. This area includes not only Lake Mead, formed by Hoover Dam, but also Lake Mohave which lies behind nearby Davis Dam. More recently, the concept of recreational areas has grown to include other lands and waters, especially in urban areas. Typical of this latter category would be the Golden Gate National Recreation Area which offers ocean beaches, redwood forests, trips to Alcatraz, coastal scenery, lagoons, marshes, and historical settings.

Are the goals of the visitors who come to recreation areas the same as those who visit national parks? From observation, it would appear that, although there are *some* common goals, there is really quite a different orientation. It seems that those who visit recreation areas do so *primarily* to escape the demands of society, of their work, or whatever is causing pressure in their lives. Consequently, there is much less interest in the more demanding walk, hike, tour, visitor center display, illustrated talk. It's enough for most people who visit recreation areas just to have some fresh air, open space, a beach to walk or lie on, a place to sit quietly in the sun and not be bothered by anyone else. Perhaps they'll be satisfied if they can go swimming, boating, hunting, picnic, fly a kite, ride a bicycle, catch a fish, watch other people.

If you're an interpreter at a recreation area, then, your goals will have to match the visitors'. For example, since swimming is such a common activity, maybe you should teach kids how to swim. Or, maybe you could help the visitor become more proficient at surf casting, fly fishing, or sailing. Maybe casual roving through the area, being as relaxed as the visitors are wanting to be, will encourage meaningful interaction with you. Perhaps it's enough for you to be satisfied with the visitor's pleasure at being at your area. If you can share a new idea or concept with the visitors as well, that's frosting on the cake.

You're not a missionary among the natives, trying to convert the public to an understanding of ecological concepts or historical relevancy—not in *blatant* ways, anyhow. Not at a recreation area especially. But, if you can be subtle, be satisfied with depositing an idea here and a concept there, you may provide a doubly useful purpose.

URBAN AREAS

The pace of life accelerates in urban areas and this affects interpretation. In these days of fast food service, condensed news via television, quick-dry clothing, radar

ranges, etc., people have become accustomed to having everything in a hurry. A need for instant satisfaction has developed in our society. All of these things affect interpretation in urban areas. Most interpretation at an urban site will have to be fast, not only because people expect it, but because crowd size demands it.

If the *majority* of your interpretation has to be fast, there won't be time for the highly-valued group interaction that's so satisfying when groups are small and in an unhurried, non-hectic environment. It means that you'll have to present your message more quickly; more concentratedly. Instead of trying to cram *everything* into the short time you have, you'll have to be selective and develop perhaps only one idea, but do it well. It'll be a challenge, considering the pressure of this kind of interpretation, to remain conversational, to adapt your message to the group, but it's still possible. You'll find some visitors who'll be interested in having an extended conversation with you, and if there aren't too many others waiting to ask you where the restroom is, you could meet their interest.

CHILDREN

In most ways, children are very much like adults. Each is a unique individual with an individual way of looking at the world. Children come to parks from a wide variety of places, having had a combination of life experiences different from anyone else's. They come with a wide variety of goals. Low on their list of priorities is the goal of being educated, receiving further schooling. They're there because one or more adult has brought them and they may feel excited and/or threatened by the absence of familiar surroundings.

Arriving at a non-urban park by automobile after hours, or days, of being cooped up in such a small environment, they'll be ready to explode into activity at the first opportunity. They have their frustrations just as adults do, but they're generally less restrained in expressing them. Children are in an intellectual growth process similar to that of adults, only it's more accelerated. The two-year difference in intellectual development between a 6-year-old and an 8-year-old is much more noticeable than the 10-year gap between a 20-year-old and a 30-year-old.

Children are generally more curious than adults. Unfortunately, many adults have become acquisitive of information rather than inquisitive as to the whys and whats of things. Children tend to be less abstract in their thought processes than adults, and often seem to have keenen senses of smell, touch, taste, and hearing. They don't know what they're supposed to experience with their senses, and thus are more open to new insights. Children, on the whole, have more lively imaginations than adults. They haven't learned what's "impossible."

A child's attention span is much shorter than an adult's, and most of them haven't learned to be politely quiet when the span is exceeded. Children are more honest and spontaneous with the expression of their feelings and, if you're sensitive, you'll know just where you stand with them. While vocabulary levels vary considerably, one of the worst things you can do to children is to talk down to them.

How can you apply the above ideas to interpretation? Here are some suggestions:

1. Since children may feel excited and/or threatened by being in a new environment, you'll need to provide a certain amount of security so the threat will subside. Your self-confidence will be a big factor in allaying fear. If your activity is well-planned, and if you share the plan with kids so they'll know what's expected, it'll be easier for them to relax. You'll probably find yourself holding hands with some of them.

2. You can capitalize on their feelings of excitement as you help them discover those things in your park area which you've decided deserve being wound up over.

3. Involve children in a variety of physical activities so they can let go of some of their pent-up energies. "Hands on" experiences and meaningful games are both good for this.

4. Make use of the uniqueness of each child. Give some of them special things to do that are related to their interests. For others, show them things that are unique to their interests. Help them be aware not only of the uniquenesses in the world around them, but the interrelationships as well.

5. Be a child yourself. That is, avoid setting yourself up as an authority figure who is going to give the children the benefit of his/her time. Have fun with the kids. Relax, be patient, encourage rather than scold.

6. Give children puzzles to work out. In an historical

setting, children could enjoy figuring out why old houses have so many chimneys, or what particular devices were used for. The Turkey Run Farm staff gives children baskets full of artifacts and, after each child has been given a silent observation period to study (feel, smell, manipulate, etc.) the contents of their container, they're asked to tell why the items were grouped together in their basket, what they have in common, etc. After examining a basket of basic food staples, for example, children are asked: Where does each item come from? How is each item obtained? How is it used? How often would it be used? How would it be stored in a cabin?

In a natural setting, children can discover the relationship of the sun to the plants which surround them, and thus to themselves, or they could discover how particular plants were named.

7. Help children develop their five senses. Give them some mint to taste. Let them smell some spices, herbs, the leather of old farm equipment. Let them feel the warmth of the ground, the prickliness of various pine needles, the softness of a Hudson Bay blanket. Provide hand lenses so kids can see another world. Listen for bird songs and marmot whistles.

8. Encourage the development of fantasy. Have them write or tell stories, compose and share poems, draw pictures. Are there any leprechauns or gremlins in your area? Could there be?

9. Use role playing as a means of interpretation for children. You'll need to give the children enough information so they can do meaningful role playing. Children can be animals, insects, rocks, the sun, whatever you and they wish.

At the Cape Cod National Seashore, children role play a sea rescue. They are first familiarized with the sea res-

cue equipment that was used 100 years ago, and then are given an imaginary training session in lifesaving. The group (which interestingly includes parents) walks to the beach and there sets up a simulated shipwreck using parents and babies as the victims out in an imaginary ship. The children "save" the women and children first and the captain last.

10. Use puppetry and other dramatization. Children like stories and when they're presented in dramatic form, they're even more likely to make a lasting impression.

11. Listen to kids. Children will appreciate having an adult listening to them without judging and putting them down. What children want to tell you may not be relevant to what you had in mind for the activity, but that doesn't matter because you've helped make it possible for the children to reciprocate by listening to you.

HANDICAPPED

Some of us play better ping pong than basketball, while others watercolor a sunset better than they swim. The amount of stamina each of us has varies considerably.

Studies show that what tastes sweet to one can taste bitter to another. And, sometimes one's inability to sense things isn't physically caused, but is determined more by cultural and/or psychological biases. Some people, blinded by their prejudices, are insensitive to anything that's contrary to their expectations. It seems safe to say that each of us is handicapped in some way.

So, the more you're able to get to know each individual visitor for whom you're interpreting, the more you can be aware of each person's handicaps and adjust to them. We tend to ignore handicapped people, to fear them, to set them apart. We can reduce this fear by reaching out to the handicapped. Make the effort to approach the handicapped to let them know you're available. They have the option of refusing your assistance, but at least you've offered. If, for example, you see a person reading a display with a magnifying glass, you might ask if they'd like you to read it for them.

Suppose a handicap requires a person to be confined to a wheelchair, and that person takes your walk or tour. What can you do to make that person feel comfortable as part of your group? Most of us like to have people look at us when they communicate, and this'll be easier if everyone's eyes are at a similar level. So, when it's appropriate to have everyone be seated, this will help equalize things for people in wheelchairs.

The basket full of artifacts exercise described as suggestion number six for children also works very well for the handicapped.

Generally speaking, if you have people with fairly serious handicaps on one of your activities, it will help if you slow the pace a bit; speak a little more loudly, slowly, clearly and simply; cover less distance; and help them understand that their handicaps don't need to make them feel all that different when they're with you.

If it's a hearing handicap, let the visitor see your face while you're talking with the group. It'll be impossible to read your lips if you have your fingers over your mouth while you talk, or if you turn your head away from the group. It'd also be helpful if you were to learn either sign language and/or finger spelling. And, by using paper and pencil you can describe more difficult concepts. It might be difficult to read your lips, for example, and get the full meaning of serotinous cones since it's hard to lip-read unfamiliar words.

Remember that even though one sense may be impaired, there are others that can be used. Find ways in which you can appeal to the other senses. When you encourage the handicapped to use more than one sense, you're also doing a favor for the more able people in the group.

I once had the experience of being the eyes for a busload of visually handicapped people for a day in Yellowstone. Although it was many years ago, I still recall vividly the experience that seemed to mean most to them. I took the group to the brink of the Upper Falls of the Yellowstone River. This activity was the most meaningful to the group, I think, because (1) they *heard* the roar of the falls and experienced its power, (2) they *felt* the spray from the falls on their faces, (3) those who had traces of vision left experienced the bright reflection of light from the water, and (4) they met the challenge of accomplishing something unusual and challenging.

Another thing that would be helpful for the visually handicapped would be to offer your arm as a physical guide. The blind don't usually need level trails. They can appreciate the challenge of an incline. Those who still have partial sight can especially benefit from an offer to use your binoculars.

Some handicaps make it difficult to express oneself fluently. It will require patience on your part, but it's essential to listen.

To sum up, do everything for the handicapped you do for all other park visitors, only more so.

SENIOR CITIZENS

Senior citizens ought to be treated like everyone else until you notice that special attention is needed. Older people don't want to be segregated, put out to pasture, be made to feel they're different.

In other cultures, older people are highly respected for the wisdom that can come from many years of varied experiences. Senior citizens are a valuable resource. Reach out to them and be rewarded.

FOREIGN VISITORS

More foreign visitors come to the United States every year and the trend is likely to continue. This means that the odds of your being of assistance to a visitor from another country continually increase. It would be ideal if you were fluent in several languages, if you had abundant interpretive literature in a variety of languages, and if you were aware of each culture's value system. In the meantime, until you learn Swahili, there are a few things it might be helpful to keep in mind.

Most other countries are ahead of us in the process of converting to the metric system. Therefore, you should become facile in the use of metrics.

In this training manual, much emphasis has been put on involvement as a means of interpretation. Other cultures are less used to this method of learning, being more accustomed to the "lecture" method. This doesn't mean we should "lecture" when we interpret for foreigners, but an awareness of the difference may help you understand why the response you receive from foreigners is less than you expect. Many foreigners like being involved, but since they've had such limited experience with it, they may feel awkward when exposed to it.

It isn't likely that you'd want to be referred to as the "typical American" when you travel abroad. You'd probably prefer to be recognized for the individual you are rather than as a stereotype. In the same way, you should avoid stereotyping others because of their nationalities. Learn to know each individual person.

It's important to recognize ethnic groups so you can relate what you're interpreting to something in their part of the world (provided your geographical knowledge is accurate). Usually, you can just ask people where they're from, and they're glad to share that information with you, but many Orientals don't like to be asked that question because they think you ought to be able to tell their ethnic group from their appearance. If you're like most Americans, you won't be able to distinguish that finely, so you'll have to beat around the bush in your conversation until the information you need comes out.

It'll be helpful to use as many visuals as you can when interpreting for foreigners. A map is a visual that seems to be universally understood.

In an emergency situation, if a visitor really needs to talk with someone who speaks his/her language, you can refer them to the International Visitor Information Service in Washington, D.C. This private, non-profit, volunteer program has a language bank of volunteers who speak nearly every language there is. The number to call is 202-872-8747. As a mnemonic device, it's interesting to note that the last seven numbers in this series, when dialed, read USA-TRIP.

MINORITY GROUPS

It's difficult to make generalizations about minorities, not only because there are so many different minorities, but also because of the danger of stereotyping. Probably the most important thing to remember is one of the primary elements of interpretation—no two people see the world the same way. Similarly, no two cultural groups see the world the same way, and members of the same minority see things differently as well. Each minority group, in general, has its own particular ways of interpreting reality, and this is often different from the views of the majority group. This causes problems everywhere in the world, and is not unique to the National Park Service.

Are there any special problems in interpretation because of the variety of ways people see the world? Of course. For example, most of the interpreters in the National Park Service are white, Anglo-Saxon protestants. In general, they have been taught to respect people

in uniform; that the policeman is a person who can help you when you're in trouble. The minority group may have been taught to steer clear of the person in uniform because you'll be hassled if you get involved. A member of the minority comes to the park area, and there you are in your uniform that looks something like a policeman's. The badge is a symbol of authority. While your uniform may be appealing to most middle-class white Americans, especially older ones, it will likely be a negative factor as far as minority groups are concerned. You'll have to do the reaching out, to let them know you're there to be of service to them.

Make an effort to get to know the value systems of other people. Become aware of your own value system and periodically question the things you tend to automatically assume to be "right." Be open to the notion that another's way of believing can be as valid as yours. You don't have to *believe* as others do, and you don't have to be wishy-washy without a point of view, but it's important to be *accepting* of life styles contrary to your own.

Avoid a patronizing missionary attitude.

When doing interpretations of historical events, it's particularly important to include the contributions of minorities, and to be aware of how they have been treated, and how they *feel* about the general American heritage. Only recently have we begun to remove, for example, those interpretive devices which gave such a one-sided view of the conflict between Native Americans and the white man.

There are other historical "minorities" as well, such as factory workers, women and children. How did factory workers feel about their working conditions? What were the effects of child labor in the family—on the children themselves? Were women workers exploited in a developing industrial society? Too often, we tell history only from the point of view of management and the successful.

[For a review of this chapter, see questions 150 through 181 in Chapter 8.]

Chapter 8

Self-Evaluation

You'll be evaluated by your supervisor(s) as well as by your peers, and occasionally you'll receive comments from park visitors, but perhaps the most important of all evaluations is the way you see yourself. Responding to the following statements may help you determine how well you're doing as an interpreter. Although the statements are arranged under various headings, they are sometimes applicable under several headings. Check the appropriate block for each statement. Then you can decide if you think improvement is necessary. You may want to ask others to give you a rating so you can benefit from a variety of points of view.

● ALWAYS　　◗ MOST OF THE TIME

◖ SOMETIMES　　◔ RARELY

GENERAL ATTITUDE　　　　　　　　　　　●◗◖◔

1. I have an insatiable curiosity. ☐☐☐☐

2. I realize that the search for knowledge is continuous. ☐☐☐☐

3. I have a love for all life. ☐☐☐☐

4. I have a high regard for the incredibly complex ecology that gives special vitality to my park area. ☐☐☐☐

5. I have an appreciation for human history of my area. ☐☐☐☐

6. I have a high regard for park visitors. ☐☐☐☐

7. I am concerned for the welfare and safety of visitors. ☐☐☐☐

8. I want visitors to be better informed, inspired and stimulated because of who I am. ☐☐☐☐

9. I want to share myself and what I know with visitors. ☐☐☐☐

10. I treat all visitors equally regardless of age, sex, race; or the way they treat me. ☐☐☐☐

11. I'm cheerful, patient and courteous. ☐☐☐☐

12. I care about my appearance and dress appropriately for my job. ☐☐☐☐

13. I don't put people down for asking "dumb" questions. ☐☐☐☐

14. I start and end all my activities on time. ☐☐☐☐

15. I reach out to people; make myself approachable, available. ☐☐☐☐

16. I believe in what I'm doing. ☐☐☐☐

17. I feel enthusiastic about my work. ☐☐☐☐

●◐◖○

18. I try to lighten my approach and use humor when it's appropriate. ☐☐☐☐

19. I'm self-confident without being conceited. ☐☐☐☐

20. I exert a quiet, gentle, but firm leadership. ☐☐☐☐

21. I can walk on water. ☐☐☐☐

UNDERSTANDING OF AUDIENCES

22. I'm aware of some of the reasons people come to my park area. ☐☐☐☐

23. I understand the processes by which people learn. ☐☐☐☐

GOALS OF INTERPRETATION

24. I understand the goals of interpretation. ☐☐☐☐

25. I'm striving to accomplish the goals of interpretation. ☐☐☐☐

PRIMARY ELEMENTS OF INTERPRETATION—INVOLVEMENT

26. I arrive at my activity early so I can become acquainted with my group. ☐☐☐☐

27. Before conducting an activity, I have always established a rapport. ☐☐☐☐

28. I'm aware that what I do first is especially important, and give it my special attention. ☐☐☐☐

29. I adapt every presentation to those in the group. ☐☐☐☐

30. I use questioning effectively as an involvement technique. ☐☐☐☐

31. I encourage visitors to use all their senses. ☐☐☐☐

32. I use a variety of structural patterns to make my presentations more involving. □□□□

ORGANIZATION

33. Every activity I conduct has a theme. □□□□

34. I select main headings which support my theme. □□□□

35. I arrange my main headings in an orderly fashion. □□□□

36. Introductions to my presentations create a favorable atmosphere and arouse interest in my subject. □□□□

37. The conclusions to my presentations inspire my audiences. □□□□

GIVING LIFE TO POTENTIALLY DULL SUBJECTS

38. I use a variety of support material that's carefully researched. □□□□

39. I tell stories, relate anecdotes, employ narration and use visuals in my presentations. □□□□

40. I'm careful to provide transitions as I move from one idea to another. □□□□

41. I select understandable words. □□□□

42. Informal, concrete language typifies my presentations. □□□□

43. My delivery is enthusiastic, self-assured and physically direct. □□□□

44. My style of delivery is friendly, pleasant, informal and casual. □□□□

45. I adapt my pace to the situation. □□□□

GIVING INFORMATION AND ORIENTATION ●◐◐○

46. I try to assess the needs of visitors and give them the amount of information I think they want. ☐☐☐☐

47. I'm convinced it's important to give accurate information. ☐☐☐☐

48. If I don't know the answer to a visitor's question, I look it up. ☐☐☐☐

49. I reach out to visitors by greeting them. ☐☐☐☐

VISITOR CENTERS

50. I give equal attention to all visitors. ☐☐☐☐

51. I don't make fun of visitors' questions. ☐☐☐☐

52. I listen to understand when I'm hearing complaints. ☐☐☐☐

53. I answer questions as if it's the first time I've been asked them. ☐☐☐☐

54. I use sketches and visuals to enhance the spoken word. ☐☐☐☐

55. I sometimes ask a visitor to paraphrase the directions I've given. ☐☐☐☐

56. I know how to read maps upside-down. ☐☐☐☐

57. I give *interpreted* facts. ☐☐☐☐

58. I'm conscious of the need to provide for the visitors' safety. ☐☐☐☐

ROVING INTERPRETATION

59. I interpret facts only when its appropriate. ☐☐☐☐

60. I sometimes gather groups for mini-walks or mini-tours. ☐☐☐☐

TALKS ●●◐○

61. I mix with the audience during the pre-talk period.
□ ▣ □ □

62. I make myself available to visitors for questions after a talk. □ □ □ □

63. When I use slides in a talk, I use them as support material, not as crutches. □ □ □ □

64. I refer to the slides directly only when there's a special reason. □ □ □ □

65. The only slides I use are those which support my theme. □ □ □ □

66. I don't use slides as cues. □ □ □ □

67. I become acquainted with my audience before the program begins. □ □ □ □

68. My campfire program doesn't run over 35 minutes.
□ □ □ □

69. I use recorded music during the pre-talk period only when it's appropriate. □ □ □ □

70. If I use community singing, I don't overdo it.
□ □ □ □

71. I use interviews and question-answer periods before the talk when appropriate. □ □ □ □

72. I keep my announcements brief. □ □ □ □

DEMONSTRATIONS

73. I make sure that what I'm showing is visible.
□ □ □ □

74. I gather the audience around me for an intimate, easily seen and heard presentation. □ □ □ □

75. My historical demonstrations are accurate, interesting and relevant. □ □ □ □

LIVING HISTORY

76. I avoid references to the present. ☐☐☐☐

77. I live my role during the time I'm in costume.
☐☐☐☐

78. I dress accurately, from the skin out. ☐☐☐☐

79. I put what I'm doing within a context. ☐☐☐☐

80. I continually study the period in which I'm taking a role. ☐☐☐☐

THE LIVING MILITARY POST

81. I understand the social structure of a military post.
☐☐☐☐

82. I realize that each post was a unique organization.
☐☐☐☐

THE LIVING FARM

83. I'm aware of the need to research farming in my period continually. ☐☐☐☐

84. I'm willing to make compromises for the sake of safety and out of consideration for neighboring farms.
☐☐☐☐

ENVIRONMENTAL LIVING

85. I present accurate, helpful material to teachers before the site visit by the students. ☐☐☐☐

86. I use environmental living to help teachers and students understand their lives against the tapestry of another culture. ☐☐☐☐

NATURAL AREA DEMONSTRATIONS

87. I use a demonstration as an "excuse" to interpret bigger concepts. ☐☐☐☐

● ● ○ ○

88. I am especially aware of feedback in this situation, as I realize I'm teaching a process. □□□□

SKY INTERPRETATION

89. I relate the sky to the earth. □□□□

90. I use sky interpretation to help people clarify their value systems. □□□□

WALKS, TOURS AND HIKES

91. I arrive at the assembly point at least 15 minutes before the activity is scheduled to begin. □□□□

92. I start on time. □□□□

93. I warn people of dangers along the way. □□□□

94. I explain the reasons for any special restrictions. □□□□

95. I move the group in a way which indicates this activity isn't going to be static. □□□□

96. I shorten the amount of material I cover when the group is larger. □□□□

97. I maintain a pace that's neither tiring nor boring. □□□□

98. I have a definite conclusion to my activity. □□□□

99. I make sure all can see and hear. □□□□

100. I avoid giving a canned spiel. □□□□

GUIDED TOURS OF HISTORICAL AREAS.

101. I emphasize relevant aspects of the area. □□□□

102. I overcome the static nature of the site by humanizing it. □□□□

●◐◑○

103. I recreate the original setting in the minds of visitors. ☐☐☐☐

104. I keep my presentation lively by giving lots of specific examples. ☐☐☐☐

105. My knowledge of the area continually grows. ☐☐☐☐

106. I adapt each presentation to the uniqueness of each audience. ☐☐☐☐

107. I put events in context. ☐☐☐☐

THE HISTORIC STRUCTURE

108. I spend time with groups before tours begin. ☐☐☐☐

109. I avoid hurrying the group through the structure. ☐☐☐☐

110. I create images of what happened within the structure. ☐☐☐☐

111. I give special attention to children who are on the tour. ☐☐☐☐

112. I help visitors imagine they're part of the scene. ☐☐☐☐

113. I share myself personally with the group and invite group members to reciprocate. ☐☐☐☐

114. I protect items of antiquity. ☐☐☐☐

THE BATTLEFIELD

115. I don't glorify war, but present the situation realistically. ☐☐☐☐

116. I help visitors visualize the event which occurred at the battle site. ☐☐☐☐

117. I give groups a geographical orientation. ☐☐☐☐

●●◑○

118. I provide a balanced and accurate account of the battle. ☐☐☐☐

THE ARCHAEOLOGICAL SITE

119. I explain why artifact collecting isn't allowed. ☐☐☐☐

120. I make it possible for visitors to compare their lives with those who once lived at this site. ☐☐☐☐

GUIDED WALKS AND HIKES IN NATURAL AREAS

121. I make sure that people know what's expected of them. ☐☐☐☐

122. I practice conservation during the activity. ☐☐☐☐

123. I handle accidents with good judgment. ☐☐☐☐

124. I'm concerned for the safety of my group. ☐☐☐☐

125. I encourage people to *experience* nature. ☐☐☐☐

126. I involve visitors in the process of learning. ☐☐☐☐

127. I look for ideas which cause people to say: "I didn't know that." ☐☐☐☐

128. I find things of special interest for children. ☐☐☐☐

129. On extended hikes, I make sure everyone is adequately clothed, equipped and physically capable. ☐☐☐☐

130. I use rest stops as interpretive opportunities. ☐☐☐☐

131. I avoid dangerous situations. ☐☐☐☐

●●●○

132. I carry first-aid materials and know how to use them. ☐☐☐☐

133. I help people understand the relationship between themselves and their environment. ☐☐☐☐

TOUR BOATS

134. I don't take advantage of the captive audience by talking too much. ☐☐☐☐

135. I visit informally with small groups on the boat. ☐☐☐☐

136. I preview what's going to happen next. ☐☐☐☐

CANOES

137. I'm concerned with safety. ☐☐☐☐

138. I plan ashore as well as afloat activities. ☐☐☐☐

139. I suggest what will be seen ahead. ☐☐☐☐

AUTO CARAVANS

140. If I'm going to use a citizen's band transmitter, I remember to talk to the group in a conversational manner. ☐☐☐☐

141. I seek feedback from the group at stops. ☐☐☐☐

142. I manage the group so as to prevent traffic hazards. ☐☐☐☐

TRAMS

143. I make myself visible. ☐☐☐☐

144. I interact with the group as much as possible. ☐☐☐☐

WINTER

145. I listen empathetically to visitors' experiences.

☐☐☐☐

146. I provide more in-depth interpretation to those who wish it. ☐☐☐☐

147. I'm willing for the scenery to speak for itself.

☐☐☐☐

148. I willingly and patiently give instruction in the use of snowshoes and skis. ☐☐☐☐

149. I'm on the lookout for weather changes that could cause hazardous conditions. ☐☐☐☐

RECREATION AREAS

150. I realize that all visitor goals don't have to be "serious." ☐☐☐☐

151. I'm satisfied if visitors find relaxation and happiness. ☐☐☐☐

152. I adapt my goals to visitors' goals. ☐☐☐☐

153. I'm subtle in the deposition of ideas and concepts.

☐☐☐☐

URBAN AREAS

154. I present material quickly, but personally and interestingly. ☐☐☐☐

155. I cover fewer ideas, but develop them well.

☐☐☐☐

CHILDREN

156. I believe that children are people. ☐☐☐☐

157. I provide a measure of security for children.

☐☐☐☐

● ◐ ○ ◌

158. I help children discover things. ☐☐☐☐

159. I regard each child as a unique person. ☐☐☐☐

160. I give children puzzles to work out. ☐☐☐☐

161. I involve children in a variety of physical activities. ☐☐☐☐

162. I assist children in the use of their senses.
☐☐☐☐

163. I encourage the development of fantasy.
☐☐☐☐

164. I use role playing and other dramatization.
☐☐☐☐

165. I listen to kids. ☐☐☐☐

HANDICAPPED

166. I realize that each of us is handicapped in some way. ☐☐☐☐

167. I get to know handicapped people personally.
☐☐☐☐

168. I adapt my activities to the handicapped.
☐☐☐☐

169. I'm aware of special techniques that are helpful for the handicapped. ☐☐☐☐

170. I listen to the handicapped. ☐☐☐☐

SENIOR CITIZENS

171. I treat senior citizens just like everyone else, unless they have a special need. ☐☐☐☐

172. I'm appreciative of the wisdom that can come from age. ☐☐☐☐

FOREIGN VISITORS

173. I avoid stereotyping foreigners. ☐☐☐☐

174. I'm familiar with the metric system. ☐☐☐☐

175. I recognize foreigners as individuals. ☐☐☐☐

176. I emphasize visuals when dealing with foreigners.
☐☐☐☐

MINORITY GROUPS

177. I avoid stereotyping minorities. ☐☐☐☐

178. I realize that minorities have played a major role in the history of this nation, but have not always been treated fairly. ☐☐☐☐

179. I'm aware that there are several valid ways to see the same thing. ☐☐☐☐

180. I'm accepting of life styles other than my own.
☐☐☐☐

181. I'm trying to be fair, accurate, unprejudiced.
☐☐☐☐

Chapter 9

Recommended Resources

COMMUNICATION THEORY

Fabun, Don. *Communications: The Transfer of Meaning.* Beverly Hills: Glencoe Press, 1968.

A concise, stimulating view of communication, written in a lively style and well illustrated.

Haney, William V. *Communication and Organizational Behavior*, 3d. ed. Homewood, Illinois: Richard D. Irwin, Inc., 1973.

Clearly explains some of the major reasons for breakdowns in human communication. Gives specific suggestions for avoiding these breakdowns.

Johnson, Kenneth G., Mark C. Liebig, Gene Minor, and John J. Senatore. *Nothing Never Happens*, teacher's ed. Beverly Hills: Glencoe Press, 1974.

A collection of exercises which promotes self-discovery. Includes thought-provoking articles. Excellent for group training.

Johnson, Wendell. *People in Quandaries.* N.Y.: Harper and Row, 1946.

A classic. Although a few of the examples are out of date, this is the best treatment of the relationship between language and behavior I know of.

Lee, Irving J. *Handling Barriers in Communication*. San Francisco: International Society for General Semantics, 1968.

A series of presentations used in training people to overcome communication barriers. Excellent for training purposes.

Postman, Neil and Charles Wingartner. *Teaching as a Subversive Activity*. N.Y.: Dell Publishing Co., 1969.

Interpretation can be thought of as a specialized form of teaching. This is my favorite book on teaching.

Rogers, Carl R. *On Becoming a Person*. Boston: Houghton Mifflin, 1961.

Developing one's self is essential to good interpretation. This book, more than any other I know, can be helpful with this.

Verderber, Rudolph F. *The Challenge of Effective Speaking*, 3d ed. Belmont, CA: Wadsworth Publishing Co., Inc., 1976.

An outstanding overview of the speaking process

RESOURCES PREPARED FOR INTERPRETERS

Alderson, William T. and Shirley Payne Low. *Interpretation of Historic Sites*. Nashville: American Assoc. for State and Local History, 1976.

The best book I know of on the subject. A must for all interpreters of historic sites.

Beechel, Jacque. *Interpretation for Handicapped Persons: A Handbook for Outdoor Recreational Personnel*. Seattle: National Park Service, Pacific Northwest Region, Cooperative Park Studies Unit, College of Forest Resources, University of Washington, 1975.

Many helpful suggestions on an important subject.

Bernard, Nelson T., Jr. (compiler). *One Step Beyond*. Southwestern Region, U.S. Forest Service, n. d.

A good, brief discussion of the interpretive walk. Contains some excellent suggestions on involving children that would work just as well for adults.

Harrison, Anne. *Interpreting the River Resource*. Washington, D.C.: U.S. Forest Service, U.S. Government Printing Office, 1977.

Knudsen, George J. *Nature Hike Themes*. Madison: Wisconsin Dept. of Natural Resources, 1976.
If you need help thinking of possible themes for your nature walk, this booklet is a goldmine of ideas.

Lewis, William J. *The Fine Art of Interpretive Critiquing*. Washington, D.C.: National Park Service, Division of Interpretation, 1975.
A series of four videotapes showing excerpts from actual interpretive activities at Independence National Park and Yellowstone National Park together with critiques of the excerpts.

National Park Service, Division of Interpretation. *A Personal Training Program for Interpreters*. Washington, D.C.: U.S. Government Printing Office, 1976.
Designed for use with or without an accompanying set of videotapes, this manual is especially helpful in the development of skills which lead to *involvement* in interpretation.

National Park Service. *Training Methods Manual: A Training Guide for Supervisors and other Instructors to Enable Them to Increase the Effectiveness of all National Park Service Training Activities*, rev. ed. Washington, D.C.: National Park Service, 1967.
Designed for supervisors and instructors, this manual can be just as helpful to the trainee.

Sharpe, Grant. *Interpreting the Environment*. N.Y.: John Wiley & Sons, Inc., 1976.
An excellent overview of the field of interpretation.

Highly recommended.

Stephenson, Lee and Nancy Strader. *Energy Workbook for Parks*. Arlington, Va.: Park Project on Energy Interpretation, National Recreation and Park Assoc., 1977.

Develops six energy themes and gives many exercises interpreters can use when interpreting energy.

Tilden, Freeman. *Interpreting Our Heritage*, 3d. ed. Chapel Hill: The University of North Carolina Press, 1977.

A classic! This book has influenced interpretation more during the last two decades than any other single source.

Van Matre, Steve. *Acclimatization: A Sensory and Conceptual Approach to Ecological Involvement*. Martinsville, Ind.: American Camping Assoc., 1972.

Acclimatizing: A Personal and Reflective Approach to a Natural Relationship. Martinsville, Ind.: American Camping Assoc., 1974.

Van Matre shows more clearly than any person I know how to develop concepts, ideas, and philosophy from one's experiences. His inductive, experiential approach is outstanding. Especially helpful are the many suggested activities.

RESOURCES WHICH COMBINE THE PHILOSOPHY OF INTERPRETATION, THE ART OF INTERPRETATION, EXCELLENT COMMUNICATIVE STYLE, AND THOUGHT-STIRRING POINTS OF VIEW.

Brown, Dee A. *Bury My Heart at Wounded Knee:* An Indian History of the American West. N.Y.: Holt Rinehart & Winston, 1970.

Brown, William E. *Islands of Hope*. Parks and Recreation in Environmental Crisis. Washington, D.C.: National Recreation and Park Assoc., 1971.

Carrighar, Sally. *One Day at Teton Marsh*. N.Y.: Ballantine Books, 1947.

Clark, Kenneth. *Civilisation:* A Personal View. N.Y.: Harper & Row, Publishers, 1969.

Dillard, Annie. *Pilgrim at Tinker Creek*. N.Y.: Harper's Magazine Press, 1974.

Dubos, Rene. *So Human an Animal*. N.Y.: Charles Scribner's Sons, 1968.

Eiseley, Loren. *The Immense Journey*. N.Y.: Vintage Books, 1957.

Everhart, William C. *The National Park Service*. N.Y.: Praeger Publishers, 1972.

Fabun, Don. *The Dynamics of Change*. Englewood Cliffs, N. J.: Prentice-Hall, 1967.

Frings, Hubert and Mable. *Animal Communication*. Waltham, Mass.: Blaisdell Publishing Co., 1964.

Leopold, Aldo. *A Sand County Almanac*. N.Y.: Oxford Univ. Press, 1949.

Lewis, Meriwether. *The Lewis and Clark Expedition*. The 1814 edition, unabridged, 3 vols. Philadelphia: J.B. Lippincott Co., 1961.

Lindbergh, A. M. *Gift from the Sea*. N.Y.: Vintage, 1965.

Sarett, Lew. *Covenant with Earth:* A Selection from the Poetry of Lew Sarett. Gainesville, Fla.: Univ. of Fla. Press, 1956.

Thomas, Lewis. *The Lives of a Cell:* Notes of a Biology Watcher. N.Y.: Bantam Books, Inc., 1971.

Toffler, Alvin. *Future Shock*. N.Y.: Random House, 1970.

THOSE WHO HELPED

Many people helped me put this book together. Primary among them is Roy Graybill, Interpretive Specialist in the Washington Office of the National Park Service. He conceived the idea of combining and updating the various National Park Service interpretive training manuals, nurtured the project over a three-year period, and brought it to fruition. I shall ever be grateful for his enthusiastic encouragement and friendship. Keith Hoofnagle's insightful drawings have strengthened the book with a light touch. His design has provided an attractive and helpful emphasis. Frank Barnes, retired National Park Service historian, was my historical consultant. His critique of my early manuscripts both sharpened my thinking, and gave me some new ways of looking at historical interpretation. Two friends, Anne Townsend and Katherine January, critiqued my writing at its various stages. Their comments enabled me to be clearer, more sensitive to a variety of issues, more accurate. More than that, their enthusiastic response encouraged me when I needed it.

During the quarter century I have been associated with the National Park Service, I have gratefully learned much from my associates, especially my Yellowstone colleagues. Three of the latter were especially helpful in preparing this book when they wrote out some ideas for consideration. They were Jim Lenertz, who wrote about the extended hike; Fred Hirschmann, winter interpretation; and Karen Chin, interpretation for the handicapped.

Al Mebane and John Tyers, Chief Park Naturalist and Assistant Chief Park Naturalist at Yellowstone during the preparation of this book, were helpful in many ways. The book was written under the guidance of the Division of Interpretation and Visitor Services, National Park Service, Washington, D.C. Dave Dame, who headed this division during the writing of this book, gave unstinting support and counsel. I also received helpful feedback from the Service's Regional Chiefs of Interpretation. I have borrowed liberally from earlier National Park Service training publications, and I'm grateful to these earlier writers.

Although I have greatly benefited from the various suggestions I have received, I am solely responsible for the selection of the material in this book.

Finally, I'm grateful to my family, especially my wife Sue, for providing me with the loving environment which made writing this book possible.

Bill Lewis

YELLOWSTONE PARK
July 1, 1980

Clickity Click

ABOUT THE AUTHOR

Bill Lewis began working for the National Park Service as a career-seasonal at Yellowstone National Park in 1949. He has continued there as a ranger and as an interpretive naturalist. In 1970, he was appointed by Yellowstone as its oral communication specialist. The new position required him to help a staff of about 55 interpreters, via various training programs and ongoing consultation during the summer months, to communicate more effectively with park visitors. The program was so successful in Yellowstone that it has been adopted throughout the National Park Service.

He has also assisted with communication training at the Mather and Albright Training Centers, Pacific Northwest Region, Mammoth Cave National Park, Grand Teton National Park, Independence National Historical Park, Boston National Historical Park, and Jasper National Park, Alberta, Canada.

In 1975–76, under a grant from the National Park Service, he visited 70 park areas from Alaska to Florida over an 8-month period to determine how energy could be effectively interpreted.

He demonstrated how to help interpreters improve their communication with park visitors in a videotape training series called "The Fine Art of Interpretive Critiquing." This National Park Service series is being used internationally to train both supervisors and interpreters.

When Bill isn't working summers for the National Park Service, he is Professor of Communication at the University of Vermont where he has worked with students since 1954. He thus combines, in this book, an academic knowledge of the theories of communication, many years of personally communicating with park visitors, and a wide experience helping other interpreters communicate more effectively.

Hoofnagle